To Kyle:

I pray that your preaching ministry will bring many souls to Christ. May He give you wisdom and strength and love!

Orita

Warren & Marilyn Meyer

*O*rita

Rites of Passage for Youth of African Descent in America

by Marilyn and Warren L. Maye

FaithWorks
New York City

Publisher's Cataloging-in-Publication
(Provided by Quality Books, Inc.)

Maye, Marilyn, (Marilyn Claire)
    Orita : rites of passage for youth of African descent in America / by Marilyn and Warren L. Maye. -- 1st ed.
      p. cm.
      Includes bibliographical references.
      LCCN: 99-
      ISBN: 0-9675400-0-3

      1. Afro-American youth--Religious life.
2. Afro-American youth--Conduct of life.
3. Puberty rites--United States. I. Maye, Warren L. II. Title.

BR563.N4M39 2000   248'.83
                 QBI99-1737

Requests for permission to make copies of any part of the work, or to order should be mailed to: Permissions, or Orders, FaithWorks, Post Office Box 144, Bronx, New York 10475-0144, USA

Printed in the United States of America by Morris Publishing, 3212 E. Hwy 30, Kearney, NE 68847, 800-650-7888

---

*This book is dedicated to our parents
and grandparents and the communities of faith,
who wouldn't give up, so we could live and thrive,
and to our son
and to all those who have gone before us
and who will come behind
seeking to fulfill their highest dreams.*

Acknowledgements

This work represents the contributions of many more than we could ever fully acknowledge.

Our *Orita* could not have been the same without the families who shared the entire experience with us: Deborah and Ashanay Bristol; Lesley, Rose, and Rodney Cummins; John, Claudia, John, and Micah Hunter; Honorable Deighton, Norma, Deighton, and Daniel Waithe; Jean and Malcolm Valz.

Special thanks to Charles, Hildred, and Duane Chinua Kwasi Thomas, who pioneered *Orita* in our circle. Our Village Elder, Honorable Carl O. Callender, and Rev. Moses Egharevba, Rev. Samuel A. Morgan, and Rev. Jabez Springer provided spiritual guidance and support. Joanne Atehka, Seon Bristol, Stella Bristol, and Daniel Diakanwa shared their time and substance with our youth. Lena Ferguson and Janice Hawkins graced our ceremony with their talents. Dr. Joyce F. Baynes, Dr. Grace Burke, Rev. Olivia Capers, Marilyn J. Holifield, Esq.,

Dr. Peter and Susan Natale, Gloria Nurse, and Dr. Mae Alice Reggy offered endless encouragement that we should document this project.

Thanks to Frieda Hale and Etta Ladson for reading the manuscript and making valuable suggestions, and to Philip Sasser for a great job on the cover.

And, of course, without the contributions of our ancestors, our communities of faith, and our God, we would have no story to tell.

Table of Contents

I loved My Africa, loved unabated
My firstborn, rocked to destiny's refrain,
When vanished from the earth are these I hated,
My Africa, preserved, shall there remain.
The continent of preservation, soil
My hand has touched, Creator foot has trod,
I am what circumstance cannot despoil,
Her Alpha Goddess and Omega God.
My first beloved daughter, rightful heir,
Her sands secure when other grounds are
charred,
Earth's holy families to her repair,
Her darkness heals the persecution scarred.
No conflagration's fire can erase
God holding Africa in Her embrace.

by Etta May Ladson, *Strange Land Songs*,
Reprinted by permission, Jewelgate Press, Publishers,
135-38 226 Street, Laurelton, New York, 11413

Fix these words of mine in your hearts and
minds; tie them as symbols on your hands and
bind them on your foreheads.
Teach them to your children,
talking about them when you sit at home and
when you walk along the road,
when you lie down and when you get up.
Write them on the doorframes
of your houses and on your gates,
so that your days and the days of your children
may be many in the land that the LORD swore to
give your forefathers,
as many as the days that the heavens are
above the earth."
—*Deuteronomy 11:18–21*
New International Version

Chapter 1

Introducing *Orita*

While deciding how to publish this book, we had a conversation about it with another author. When he heard the topic, he predicted, "you're only going to interest black folks who are Afro-centric in their thinking. That's a very small percentage of the marketplace."

Whether you consider yourself Afro-centric or not, this book is for you. You don't have to wear African attire or give your child an African name (although we have done both), to find value in these pages. Whatever your political views, your religious practices, or the kind of neighborhood you live in, we invite you to consider adopting the practice described here, as an investment in the future of your children.

We have written this book, to help establish a new tradition for descendants of the African Diaspora. More accurately, we write to re-establish and update an ancient tradition, so that it works here and now

5

and for the future.

We hope that, after reading further, you'll want to join us in this effort.

Maybe you're a parent, grandparent, godparent, aunt or uncle, stepsibling, or any adult who has a close personal relationship with a girl or boy of African descent.

You may be a youth who wants to know more about what is expected of you when you become an adult.

Maybe you've seen one too many a bright, promising, black child fall short of his or her potential, or worse. You want to be a part of the solution, rather than the problem.

Maybe you're sick and tired of the victim role. Instead of focusing on our suffering from individual and institutional racism, you want to pass on a more empowering legacy to your children and to the youth of your community.

Perhaps you're familiar with initiation rites for young people, but want more information about how to participate in one.

Whichever your reason, we invite you to read on, to consider adopting the tradition, and to help us spread the word. The word is "*Orita*".

"*Orita*" celebrates the coming-of-age of youth of African descent. "*Orita*" is about acknowledging and generating success in spite of obstacles, ensuring and celebrating our permanence and durability, generation after generation. Every time one of our sons or daughters crosses over successfully from childhood to adulthood, we get another opportunity to celebrate. He or she defied the odds and is contributing to a better tomorrow, for the whole planet! Every time *Orita* happens, the conversation about us among ourselves and outside of the community changes for the better. The odds move more in our favor.

"*Orita*" is an opportunity to make life better for our youth than has been for us. The *Orita* process helps prepare each youth that participates to make a difference in his or her community. At the *Orita* celebration, the community acknowledges and affirms each youth and celebrates who we are as a people.

How does "*Orita*" accomplish all this?

An alternative conversation
"*Orita*" provides a positive conversation, an alternative to the negative one our youth engage in and hear about themselves most of the time.

Popular psychology warns that our self-talk has a strong influence on who we become. "*Orita*" uses the discipline of study and the affirmation of community to reinforce a different kind of conversation from what inevitably "plays" inside the heads of black children who grow up in America, and similar environments.

Consider that growing up as an American of African descent has been and will continue to be, well

7

into the third millenium A.D., one of the biggest challenges faced by any type of American. Even when your great-grandchild will have impressive personal achievements, it will be a long time before Americans will consider his ethnic origins, and assume he will succeed and express surprise when he fails. Consider that this will not happen until we ourselves begin to think that way.

You probably don't remember a specific moment when you crossed over that big intersection which took you from being a child to becoming an adult, but somewhere during that process, it probably hit you, "something's wrong!" You began to notice that America thinks there's something wrong with being black, and you probably started deciding how that would affect what you think about yourself. One day, being black became equated, in your mind, with being stopped, being unexpected or with facing an extra hurdle - while being white was equated with access or privilege or expectation.

If you were "made in America," you know how confusing it can be, trying to figure out, usually with little good guidance, how to respond to all the challenges of growing up black in this country. *"Orita"* helps eliminate a lot of the confusion created by the feeling that "something's wrong." *"Orita"* can provide a roadmap, removing much of the guesswork about how to respond to those challenges. *"Orita"* can give our youth a realistic, empowering and optimistic framework for facing and shaping their future. How does "*Orita*" help the family and the community? We parents, caregivers, teachers and leaders agonize about how to help our children cope and thrive. We've tried integration and separation, confrontation and isolation, education and assimilation, and even denial, only to be frustrated when we see our children not taking full advantage of their God-given talents, still bowed by discrimination. "*Orita*" helps ensure the on-going health of our community, by taking a stand for our own values, in defiance of values in the larger society that devalue our contribution.

The idea of "*Orita*" was passed on to us from Rev. Frank T. Fair, author of *Orita for Black Youth: An Initiation Into Christian Adulthood*. In this manual, he documented the program that he, his wife, and congregation had sponsored, as his sixteen-year-old son faced the challenge of manhood. They adopted a Yoruba word, "*Orita*", which means "crossroads", to name their project. We liked the word "*Orita*" as soon as we heard it. Since we don't understand the Yoruba language, it sounded to us like a good word for a code - a secret password for a counterplot to foil the plans of the enemy to destroy our black boys! A code word to use along an Underground Railroad track to guide our sons to freedom. A light of hope went on. At last, here's something we can do besides wring our hands and complain about the situation, something proactive, positive and risk-free.

When we discovered "*Orita*", our own son was only a preschooler, too far from the "crossroads" of awakening to what Drs. Nathan and Julia Hare, in their manual, Bringing the Black Boy to Manhood: The Passage, call, his "racial and manhood identity". Even though our son was too young, one of our godsons was at the perfect age, and his parents were just as enthusiastic and agreed to work with us to try it out. So, he was first in our circle of acquaintances, and about eight years later, our son and six more boys followed, and the response has been so enthusiastic, that this book is the result.

Long before we encountered "*Orita*", we were aware that coming-of-age ceremonies and rituals have been practiced among all cultures, since ancient times. What has been surprising to us is discovering growing interest in these practices in our generation, even among people of European descent in the United States and Canada.

Modern life is changing so rapidly that individuals and families increasingly feel the need to have definitions that clarify even the basics of living. Self-help books, like modern Bibles, help us recover and retain our lost self-esteem. National rites-of-passage conferences are held. California foundations sponsor group initiation ceremonies for girls and their families. In a world transformed by technology, what does it mean to be female? to be adult? to be of African descent in America?

Caution: we believe an *Orita* project would be good for your son or daughter, young relative, student or other youth in your care, but you may have to do some work on yourself first. Even in writing this book, we unearthed quite a personal struggle with our own self-esteem and self-talk. Consider looking at how you feel about being an African-American adult? If you don't feel good about it, and don't believe it's worth the effort, how can you generate excitement in your youth about getting there successfully? If you're depressed and negative or in denial yourself, you're hardly going to catch the vision of what's possible for our youth in the future. This is about your child, or your charge, doing better than you've done - spiritually, emotionally, intellectually, physically, financially, in every way. It's about others building on your contribution and taking it to the next level.

This guide is simple to follow, and will not only explain how the process works, but will give you actual material that you can use or adapt for your program. We have high hopes, not only for you and your children or community, but for folks of African descent worldwide, in a ripple effect, such as:

- more and more people becoming aware of the value of *Orita* rites of passage in preparing youth of African descent for successful adulthood
- increased positive involvement and support from

adults of African descent in the lives of our youth
* more and more parents and leaders getting involved and creating *Orita* rites of passage across the African Diaspora
* artists and entrepreneurs developing materials, artifacts, and celebration items to benefit community businesses and promote economic ventures

Just imagine, if every black youth in America today had the experience of being involved in an effective *Orita* experience, what an impact this would have on the quality of family life and communities and nations led by future generations of youth of African descent.

We believe that *Orita* projects are most effective if they involve a group of youth of the same age from families in the same community. With this format, the youth can readily meet for fellowship and accountability. However, *Orita* rites for a single youngster in a family can also be effective, if planned and executed with care and creativity. And, an experience that involves youth who live in different neighborhoods or towns, and who gather periodically for the project can also provide a lasting and powerful influence on those participants.

Orita Overview
Figure 1 presents a timetable, modeled on the *Orita* rites of passage our family was involved in:

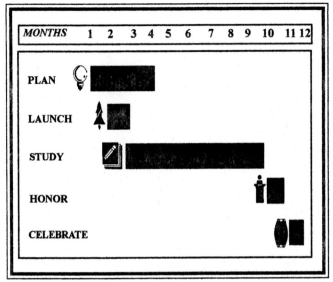

Figure 1

In the year when most of the youth will have their 12th birthdays, begin the process, and plan to celebrate the passage in the following year.

Step 1) PLAN:

Kick-off the process with a planning meeting. Gather interested parents of youth in their passage year to discuss ideas. Distribute this book to all interested parents BEFORE the first planning session. The agenda for the first meeting might be:

a) our vision

b) assignments

c) timeframe

d) next planning meeting(s)

Planners, as a group or in teams, will meet several times, to set up project schedules, gather materials, secure funds, facilities and services, plan and coordinate rites-of-passage events.

Step 2) LAUNCH

Conduct a brief launch ceremony, with the "Village Elder" presiding. (See Chapter 3).

Step 3) STUDY

During the school year, on weekends, holidays, or after school, coordinate the study component, where youth read, participate in workshops and mentoring, take trips, study, conduct interviews, prepare speeches and written material, and face physical challenges

Step 4) HONOR

Conduct the formal *Orita* rites-of-passage ceremony; honor and accept the youth as young adults in the community.

Step 5) CELEBRATE

Celebrate your youth's successful completion of *Orita* requirements and arrival at adulthood.

The requirements for developing such a rites-of-passage process are minimal. If you can plan and organize a community or social event, then you can organize an *Orita* experience for your young person. Here are the basics:

1) A responsible individual or group:

A church, school, community group, group of families or a single family may sponsor an *Orita* rites of passage.

2) A place to meet:

The sponsors should arrange to have scheduled access to a suitable facility for a series of meetings. A room big enough to arrange like a classroom is best, for the study component workshops. It should be located convenient to public transportation, automobile or walking, depending on the needs of the participants, parents, and guest speakers / presenters. If it is possible, find a donor to make the space available free of charge or at low cost. A church school or community center classroom facility is ideal. (In some circumstances, space in a home may be suitable, if a classroom atmosphere can be maintained, free of distractions.)

3) A place for the ceremony and celebration:
The sponsoring group should also arrange to use a suitable facility - auditorium AND social hall or outside area - for the passage celebration. Again, it should be located where it is accessible to families and guests. On whatever scale the celebration is conducted, it must be clear to all participants and guests that this is a very special, family affair, of deep social and spiritual significance, perhaps just less pivotal than a wedding celebration.

4) A serious attitude:
Every effort must be made to reinforce the seriousness of the commitment to study and prepare for the passage to adulthood. Some ways to communicate this are the following: seriousness about scheduling and not canceling meetings at the last minute; operating meetings / classes within planned start and end-

ing times; youth and adults faithfully preparing for and carrying out assignments, even though there are other important school and church commitments during the year.

5) Some outdoor activity:
In addition to intellectual development, some aspects of the experience should include development of spiritual, physical, and social skills. Activities outside of the classroom setting must support this.

6) A spiritual commitment:
The experience must include a significant spiritual component, rooted in worship of God, faith in one's future destiny, and adherence to scriptural teachings, principles, and lifestyle.

7) A positive perspective on our African origins and destiny:
The program should place a significant emphasis on the unique opportunities and challenges of growing up as a black adult in a multicultural world.

These 7 factors are all you really need. What you do NOT want are unnecessary or wasteful components, which complicate, distract from and undermine the spirit of your program. For example, it is NOT necessary for the program to have any of the following:

1) a budget that the families involved cannot afford, or have to go into debt or seek corporate financing to pay for;

2) self-appointed professionals to lead, instruct, or

authorize the *Orita* training and celebration;
3) the sanction of a religious organization or denomination.

So what's keeping you from getting on with it? Your youth are getting older every day and society is becoming more and more hostile to their spiritual well being. If you don't usher them safely into adulthood, they'll get there anyway, and maybe not safely.

If you are already convinced, you may elect to skip over chapter 2, which gives the case for observing rites of passage, and go straight to chapter 3 - "Mobilizing for *Orita* Rites of Passage." And, if you're already gung-ho, and need no reassurance right now that you are capable of organizing your own project, then you may want to begin with chapter 4, "Planning your *Orita* project". Perhaps, later on, in midstream, you may experience some self-doubt and may find Chapter 2 a timely source of encouragement.

The authors are so committed to seeing this practice institutionalized among black families across America, that we are seeking ways to facilitate consultation and support for families in the future. Look for our homepage on the Internet **http:// members.aol.com/orita1** for up-to-date information.

Chapter 2:

Embracing Rites of Passage

We Americans will celebrate a birth, a birthday, a graduation, a wedding, and even moving into a new home! With the exception of the birthday, these are examples of accomplishments which people work toward and decide to achieve. And, being success-oriented, we want to applaud individual achievement. We want to say "you can make it in your new status, we're behind you!" And, we want to make sure that everyone else who's thinking about doing the same thing can depend on being celebrated in the same way, if they also take the plunge.

But, can you imagine how most people would

react if you sent them an invitation to celebrate less public milestones such as: the end of your child's potty training, your daughter's first menstrual cycle, first signs of your son's facial hair or changing voice, the completion of your menopause or your graying or balding head? Your friends would probably think you had completely lost your mind! Yes, you or your relative may have reached a significant milestone in his or her life, but most people in our society are uncomfortable discussing such things with anyone at all, much less celebrating them publicly.

And, even if we're not embarrassed by such a physical change, it doesn't seem to warrant celebration. After all, we reason, it took no special talent or effort to achieve this; nobody wins a prize for it; and, what choice did the person have anyway? The transition is unavoidable.

But people have not always thought this way. In other societies and in other periods of human history, people weren't as uncomfortable about these life transitions. In fact, they embraced life cycle changes, made special preparation for and celebrated them - no stigma attached. Moving to a new life stage was often associated with honor, the favor of God, fulfilling one's purpose in life, or gaining new privileges and responsibilities in society. Social recognition and approval offset any physical discomfort. People could actually look forward to transitions, because of the promise of new status afterward. People had faith in their vision of the next life phase.

This book is based on the premise that our youth of African descent in America today not only can benefit from but also desperately need formal preparation for and celebration of their transition to adulthood. We believe they need the experience of *Orita*, whether or not they show signs of having special problems. Why? We've identified a whole list of good reasons, which we would ask you to consider more fully in the sections that follow.

Reason for *Orita* #1: Nature and Faith Call Us to Acknowledge the Future

If the Creator meant for it to be a private matter when people make the transition from child to adult, it's strange that the process is as visible as it is. The human body is programmed to change very dramatically, with dozens of physical alterations. It looks to us that it was meant for people to stop and take notice. You notice the coming of spring and start to celebrate, anticipating the changes ahead, don't you? Just as nature calls to our attention that it is waking up after winter, so when a youth blossoms, the changes beg for notice, applause and adjustment.

Whereas in most ancient societies and traditional cultures, boys and girls began to assume significant adult responsibility upon reaching puberty, modern Americans create a stage we call adolescence that lasts for six or seven years. Youth must wait all that time before we welcome them as legal and moral adults, prohibited, for example, from the right to drive, to vote, to marry, or to be held liable for contracts or for the well-being of others. Well, we can't explain how we got so out of step with nature and our foreparents, but out of step we surely are. It's as if our society is in doubt about or has no faith in what Nature is clearly saying is so.

Unfortunately, for too many boys and girls, this is a time of terrible ambivalence. Our society gives no reward or benefit to offset the discomfort of puberty. On one hand, their bodies are changing uncontrollably and often embarassingly. Breasts are growing too quickly or too slowly, hair is showing up in new places, voices crack unpredictably, and new bodily functions reveal themselves unexpectedly and in the most humiliating ways. Emotionally, young people are developing their first strong interests in and opinions about various subjects and activities. Physically and mentally, youth are developing into adults, but socially, little has changed to acknowledge that they are no longer children. Sadly, some never make the transition to becoming responsible adults; instead social welfare and criminal justice systems guide them throughout their lives.

Perhaps we are more optimistic about transitions in nature than those in human beings. As soon as the first signs of spring appear, we begin planning to enjoy and take advantage of the season changes ahead. At the early signs of our youth's passage, however, we show little excitement about their imminent adulthood. To remedy this, an *Orita* experience for each girl or boy in transition, is a statement of faith in his or her future. We celebrate because God is about to unfold His unique purpose for his or her adult life, and we expect the world to benefit from that purpose!

Reason for *Orita* #2: It's a proven strategy for continuation of the social order

Most Americans probably do not realize that the popular extreme sport called "bungee jumping" originated as an initiation into manhood for boys of the South Pacific islands nation known today as the Republic of Vanuatu. After first passing several verbal and physical tests, community leaders would require the young candidates for manhood to build a high tower of bamboo, select a strong vine, and cut it at exactly the correct length, so that when tied to the ankle, the boy's height and the remaining length of vine would cause his head to just brush the ground when he jumped from the tower. The boy's life depended upon his selecting the best vine and cutting it to the exact length. One inch too long could mean a broken neck after the bungee jump. In their society, in addition to courage and physical strength, readiness for manhood required maturity, accuracy, carefulness, and the ability to learn from one's elders.

From the South Pacific to North America,

23

from ancient to modern times, just about every society has traditionally had some formal way to mark the transition to adulthood for boys, if not also for girls. Since rituals, in general, re-affirm the social order and ensure its continuance, by rituals of the transition from childhood to adulthood, society passes on its spiritual beliefs, how the sexes are viewed, the community's history and values. These 'rites of passage', as anthropologists call them, define how a man is different from a boy, how a woman is different from a girl, and how a man is different from a woman. Since the type of rituals depended on the competencies, which were important to prepare youth for adulthood in their society, each different culture has had its own style.

The ancient rituals and ceremonies were vivid and unforgettable experiences, both for the participants and for any observers, especially younger children anticipating their future participation. Commonly, the youth would go through 'initiation', some period of preparation, training or testing, after which would be a public acknowledgment or demonstration that they had successfully completed the requirements for adulthood. For example, during the preparation phase, girls or boys might have their hair cut; be given special accessories to wear; be required to learn and perform complicated dances; have noses pierced or genitals circumcised.

Some peoples required boys to prove physical courage and skill. Boys might have to hunt certain animals; be forced to fast for a period of time; and, one group in the Americas had boys tied in a bed of ants and forced to endure ant bites. Some rituals memorialized ancestors; many initiated boys into secret societies claiming knowledge of the secrets of manhood. Some rituals required boys to show that they can function effectively in isolation from society, some rituals emphasized the requirement for teamwork and cooperation with peers.

Some of these rituals were so cruel as to be revolting to people in modern society. Perhaps those extreme cases have given a bad reputation to all rituals commemorating youth's transition to adulthood. To some, the concept seems out-of-date and simplistic. Americans typically pride ourselves on being 'non-traditional', free from the 'tyranny' of customs and ceremonies. This attitude is seen in today's tendency to eliminate or trivialize even such nearly universal rituals as marriage or mourning.

Contemporary Strategies Have
Proven Useful to Many
In recent years, some Americans of European descent have renewed their interest in rites-of-passage practices. *Crossroads: The Quest for Contemporary Rites of Passage* reflects this development, in a collection of some fifty articles assembled by researchers Mahdi, Christopher and Meade. For example, wilderness pro-

grams prepare youth for a period of physical privation, usually alone, where they discover inner strength,
answers to critical life issues, and are celebrated when
they successfully return to their community. Many
have borrowed and customized rituals from Native
American and African societies. Proponents have
organized national conferences, school curricula,
foundations, and mental health and other programs
of healing, to promote and implement this approach
to supporting contemporary youth.

Among African Americans today, numerous
individuals and organizations have begun to sponsor
rites-of-passage programs with aims similar to those
of *Orita.* Educator, Dr. Jawanza Kunjufu, is a long-
time advocate of African Americans practicing rites
of passage, and through his publishing house, African-American Images, in Chicago, has produced several volumes about such programs, some of which
are cited in our bibliography. Increasingly, in urban
and suburban communities, educational institutions
are sponsoring rites of passage for youth of various
ages, from puberty to late adolescence.

Between the mid-seventies and the nineties,
Gail Sheehy wrote several best-selling books, starting with *Passages: the Predictable Crises of Adult
Life*, which popularized the notion that even adults,
not just adolescents and children, need guidance to
successfully navigate the crossroads of life. She used
the label "passage" to describe the turning points that

mark the end of one stage and the beginning of the next. Ms. Sheehy observed that her generation faced a void, needing "a guide" to clarify what was happening in their lives, and what could be expected as they matured. If Ms. Sheehy's largely privileged subjects faced this need, how much more the youth of ethnic and socio-economic groups, about whose passages few, if any, positive books are written?

In her books, Sheehy used metaphors to try to demystify and provide a guide to otherwise uncharted and unpredictable adulthood experiences. According to her, teenagers are "Pulling Up Roots"; those in their thirties are "Rooting and Extending"; people in their forties she calls "Integrators"; fifty-year olds are on "The Rebound"; sexagenarians are in "The Second Wind". These verbal metaphors provide mental images that can help readers remember what they should expect and how they might respond.

Our ancestors also used metaphors, but these were more often non-verbal. They used symbols and dramatic rituals, which must be repeated year after year, to create strong memories to guide their youth. What could be a more powerful way to transmit social guidance than meaningful, life-size, public ritual? Cut off from our ancestral origins by the Middle Passage and slavery, most African-Americans are unable to identify the rituals which enriched our foreparents lives. *Orita* is an attempt to reconstruct this valuable aspect for our future generations.

Researchers have not yet proven the widespread value of contemporary strategies for supporting youth in their transition to responsible adulthood. Lathardus Goggins II, in his *African Centered Rites of Passage and Education*, reported positive early results from a new, African centered rites of passage program at Kent State University. African American freshmen initiated to the university through the program were demonstrating stronger academic performance than those who were not. In American society at large, in too many cases, youth are only introduced to such experiences when they are in trouble or at grave risk of failure. It will take long-term studies to definitively prove their value; can you afford to wait until that is done before taking action for your youth? We think not.

Reason for *Orita* #3: Youth create rituals when adults fail to -
On a crowded subway car in New York City, we heard a group of teenagers reviewing, as though studying for an exam, what amounts of jail time they could expect for different kinds of crimes. They were well versed in prison life routines, how many phone calls a prisoner can make, how often visitors can come, and the like, learned from the experiences of older siblings, neighbors, relatives and friends.

In many urban communities in the 1990's, the street culture marks the passage to irresponsible adulthood, through the rituals of going to prison, for boys, and of giving birth to a baby, for girls. Gang activity and rituals are resurgent generation after generation in our urban centers.

Even for youth in more upwardly-mobile communities, the self-styled rituals may include practicing tobacco, alcohol or drug abuse; sexual promiscuity, attempting death-defying feats; flagrantly violating social norms and taboos; or any variety of dysfunctional behaviors which they associate with being "grown up". Even suicide is becoming epidemic among certain young people—a rite of passage?

Whether the community idolizes the streetsmart hustler, the macho tough guy, the super-confident businessman, the athlete who'll even cheat to win, or the red-hot lover, the young men will devise ceremonies, sometimes called 'pseudo rites of passage', to show that they are ready for that adult image.

Why do we need to create an *Orita* ritual? One of the most compelling reasons is because there's a great void in our communities where strong images of responsible adulthood should be. Because too many of our people are cynical, angry and agnostic, rather than having faith in the over-arching destiny planned for us by God Himself. And, in this void, youth are either developing negative concepts of what grown-up behavior is and acting out damaging rituals to prove their manhood and womanhood, or they're rejecting growing up altogether, engaging in self-destructive behavior that will result in certain, early death.

Youth Rituals Try To Compensate
for Weak Parenting
How did this void develop? The Professors Hare have between them doctorates in psychology, sociology, and education. In their book on rites of passage, they cite a number of contributing problems in our community, one of which is the loss of parenting skills. Increasingly the products of broken or two-working parent homes, black parents today have to turn to books rather than rely on their own memories of what good parents do on a daily basis.   Single mothers worry about their sons not having daily role models of a man in the home. Increasingly, poor mothers have their children taken away from them by the social welfare system, because of parenting failures. To a large extent today, the quality of parental influence is poorer.

The rise of gang activity is another symptom of failed parenting. In the Crossroads collection, Mahdi, et. al. refer to "unparented people", found among a wide cross-section of cultural groups. They describe gang activity as one of many types of dysfunctional, dependent relationships that are often a substitute for defective or missing parent-child relationships. Instead of youth at puberty gradually and naturally letting go of dependence on their parents, youth join gangs as if seeking for what they could not depend on their parents to provide. Some never achieve adult independence, continuing gang activity well into their twenties and thirties. Beyond the family, other adult caregivers often fail to affirm a common set of values. Some trusted adults act inappropriately, teasing, insulting or even sexually abusing youth as they develop into adolescence. Some teachers and public figures champion alternative lifestyles and encourage adolescents to adopt different sexual orientations, regardless of their sexual identity. And, most adults give no input at all, unsure about what to say or do to be affirming and helpful, and what not to say or do that could be damaging.

Youth Rituals Try to Compensate
for an Ambivalent African-American Identity
Another aspect of the void comes from lack of agreement about what it means to be an African American today. African Americans in the media peddle a whole range of stereotypes, which vie for adoption by our adolescents. Then among relatives and friends, youth hear a number of conflicting messages: "I don't know anything about Africa, my parents came from America (Caribbean, Latin America)". "We should learn to blend in with white Americans, instead of separating ourselves." "We never discuss race at home." "We should learn Swahili and Yoruba, and get rid of Euro-

pean, slave names". "We are black first, and anything else second".

Such unclear messages provide poor guidance for our children, as they develop "racial identity"— the "process", according to psychologist Dr. Beverly Tatum, in her insightful work, *Why Are All the Black Kids Sitting Together in the Cafeteria?" And Other Conversations About Race*, "of defining for oneself the personal significance and social meaning of belonging to a particular racial group." Teens generally seek to define themselves in a manner that will empower them for the future, and they need adults to support them in achieving this goal. Instead, too often, youth find adults weakened by ambivalence about their African-American identity.

By contrast, if we are to prepare our children to deal effectively with a stubbornly "race-conscious society", to use Dr. Tatum's term, more of us will have to adopt and communicate empowering interpretations of our racial identity. We believe that these will be most lasting if rooted in common experiences, on which we base our identity. Two sources of such commonality are our African heritage and our spiritual one.

Orita rites of passage attempt to fill a void in our youth's consciousness by placing the spotlight on Africa. We believe that a tradition will not last long that is not tied to a common place of origin. To that end, we must root out ignorance of Africa. Our children will meet and communicate with other descendants of the African Diaspora, whose families have lived for generations in the Northern or Southern United States, the Caribbean, Canada, South America, or Europe. In spite of the diversity of cultural influences, only in the African continent can we find a place to which future generations can return for information and affirmation. Our youth must understand that there were traditional value systems, practiced before the North American slave trade, which proved critical to the survival of Africans here. The *Orita* study component provides an opportunity for our youth to discover such information.

Orita rites of passage affirm the participants' faith in the empowering message of Jesus Christ, a message that brings hope and understanding regarding the events of history. As Christ's suffering resulted in human redemption, so the peculiar suffering of people of African descent in America has had a redemptive effect, uniquely qualifying us to provide global leadership. For example, Dr. Martin Luther King, Jr. earned the Nobel Peace Prize after decades of activism for human rights, in the face of racism, injustice and terrorism. But, more than a redemptive effect, our youth also learn from the Christian message that there is a destiny for every person and for every nation, a destiny that makes sense sometimes only in God's timetable. It is only when our young people have such a theology to explain our place in the universe that they will fully embrace their black identity and the noble destiny associated with it. *Orita* rites picture a positive future for people of African descent, a future worthy of the sacrifices of responsible adult living.

Youth Rituals Compensate for Not Learning from Adult Failures

Youth can benefit from lessons learned by adults who have experienced failure. Adults can create rituals of transition as an effective way to prevent youth from repeating their mistakes.

Youth are not the only ones who need help to make the transition to the next phase of their lives. People at all ages of life suffer from the absence of meaningful rituals and of a hopeful picture of the future. We all know the story about the man facing midlife in crisis, who, seeking reassurance that he still has manly appeal, has an adulterous fling with a woman younger than his daughter, and winds up making a complete mess of his life. Because we know of people who did not make it safely from one stage to another, many of us see life transitions as "crises". Life transitions can be dangerous and scary at any age; failure is a real possibility. Sometimes, we're just not ready and don't know how to get ready?

So many adults today spend major periods of their lives in cycles of addiction and recovery, wouldn't it make sense to have many more programs to prevent than to cure these tendencies? In the Cross-roads collection, educator and transpersonal psychologist, Christina Grof describes observations frequently made by psychologists and clergypersons. She points to the great hunger that people have for "something missing in their lives", for "something more than this", a "non-specific craving" for ultimate meaning, that they later find in the loving support of church or recovery communities. When community is not accessible, individuals need to have a personal reservoir of "emotional strength." Thom Hartmann, in *Beyond ADD*, and Lathardus Goggins II, in *African Centered Rites of Passage and Education*, speak about youth needing to understand the probability of pain, to have a repertoire of empowering thoughts and understandings about themselves and other people. When life circumstances arise, the unconscious mind has a store of alternative interpretations it can tap to open possibilities for new, positive responses. Experiences like *Orita*, which acknowledge such fundamental needs of young people in transition, can put in place for youth what has been left out by their families' failure to participate meaningfully in communities and disciplines of faith.

Even if your adolescent son or daughter is not likely to succumb to destructive habits, he or she probably has a legitimate yearning for an extraordinary challenge. Young people want to be stretched to discover their potential. Youth want to know how tough they can be, or strong, courageous, responsible or any other attribute they associate with being a grown-up.

Youth Cannot Teach Youth How
To Become Responsible Adults - It's Up to Us
To support our youth and while reducing their vulnerability to destructive practices, our community needs to develop formal rituals, which preserve the collective wisdom from our experience in America and transmit it to our youth. This wisdom must clearly affirm what our community values in a man or woman. It must provide answers to questions such as, "how does a man (/ woman) respond to a challenge?" "what is success?" "what is beauty?" "what is my responsibility to my family and my community?" "how do I respond to racism?" "what is my heritage, my potential, my destiny?" And this wisdom must be transmitted in crystal clear images, which are activated as strong memories in moments of crisis and decision.

African-American adults can use *Orita* rites of passage to address the void left by weak parenting. Until we adults organize experiences like *Orita*, as long as youth desire to prove their readiness for manhood or womanhood, they will develop their own rituals based on whatever images of adulthood are most meaningful to them. Often these images are based on negative role models in their lives or in the media. Socially and morally unacceptable outcomes will result.

**Reason for Orita #4: There are benefits
for everyone, and it's FUN!**

Perhaps you feel your children or other youth are protected, are not at high risk of negative outcomes. You have a strong and supportive family background, you live in an affluent neighborhood, and your kids are active in a well-financed church. How can special rituals add value with all you've got going for you?

Think for a moment about how much more seriously people take the new status of the couple who has gone through a wedding ceremony rather than just moving in together, the student who has received his or her degree rather than being totally self-taught, the professional or tradesperson who has become licensed by the state rather than simply knowing his or her trade. There's something about openly committing to a course of preparation, submitting to the discipline and completing all the requirements, that makes people take you more seriously and makes everyone want to celebrate.

In the same way, while the chances are great that if your family, community and spiritual support structure is strong, that your child will develop into a responsible adult at some point anyway, there are several advantages of your young person committing to a formal, public process like *Orita*. 1) Since the *Orita* experience is structured, follows a timetable, requires discipline and evaluation, both the participant and the community will take it more seriously that the young person has a new status of "man" or "woman".

2) The celebration of passage into manhood or womanhood will generate numerous good memories of accomplishment, social recognition and pride.

3) Youth acquire photographs, scrapbooks, medallions and other memorabilia, which certify their completion of the preparation component. If retained, these articles will provide lasting reminders of the *Orita* principles, for frequent reflection and review.

4) As more youth engage in the *Orita* experience, younger children will look forward to participating when they get older; *Orita* will become a personal milestone, and young people will have a greater investment in their future as a "responsible adult".

5) The *Orita* experience requires that youth study their personal, family and community history. In their ordinary school, church and community activities, the focus is usually on studying other histories: of the world, the nation, the town, the faith. Doing personally relevant research, an *Orita* requirement, may very well heighten the young person's interest in other academic work. What better way to gain insight and understanding of black history and culture than by researching your own genealogy, family history and origins; interviewing elders who have survived slavery, Jim Crow, colonialism and racism; travelling to places where your foreparents grew up? Sometimes, just knowing the names and stories of your foreparents can provide motivation in facing the struggles of life;

it's harder to give up when you think of yourself as a link in a very long chain of overcomers.

6) How often do youth and adults have serious discussions about the roles of men and of women in society? Because of heightened awareness of gender discrimination and inequity in many important institutions, American society has moved away from single-sex organizations. However there is still a need for men and women to gather with others of their own sex, for principled and responsible activities, which reinforce their contribution to society. By having separate *Orita* projects for boys and for girls, youth gain an opportunity to explore in depth the roles of men and women in society, topics, which are rarely addressed in traditional church, family and community forums.

Orita for boys should present and model manhood as more than physical power or sexual capability, but as a status based on response-ability - i.e. ability to respond in situations, to needs, to the people in their lives. As they get to spend time socially and recreationally with responsible men who can give constructive feedback, boys can practice manliness during the *Orita* experience.

Orita for girls can focus on the wide variety of options which women now have for reaching their potential. Your program should introduce the girls to black women who are the best models of godly womanhood, rather than women whose low self-esteem invites victimization and abuse.

7) Commitments made during the program may act as a deterrent to making bad decisions in a moment of choice.

There are benefits also for those who attend or participate in preparation for the formal event.

8) At the celebration, adults as well as peers of the youth from the community get a singular opportunity to observe the talents and interests of the youth in the program.

9) Adults get to share gifts and words of appreciation with their youth, which might never otherwise be shared.

10) Adults get to know the youth better, by name and by their individual interests and achievements, as they participate in public rituals celebrating their transition to adulthood. Just think what the ripple effect would be on a neighborhood; adults and youth would team up to help each other a lot more often, rather than being adversaries as is so often the case.

11) Religious communities may benefit from the *Orita* experience's impact on their youth's spiritual development. We should note that *Orita* is not a substitute for baptism, confirmation, or any religious rituals or sacraments practiced by communities of faith. Those rituals signal the believer's transition to spiritual maturity in the faith. Although not exclusively for adolescents, Catholic and Protestant confirmation ceremonies and Jewish bar and bat mitzvah services are

traditionally conducted as their youth enter their teenage years.

However, the majority of black families in America do not belong to religious traditions, which practice such rituals. And, even for those that do observe such traditions, the ceremonies are often steeped in untranslated, European cultural practices, which make it harder for African-American youth to integrate the rituals into their experience of growing up in this culture.

So, increasingly today, families of African descent, whatever their religious faith, are turning to tailoring customs and devising rituals, which combine many of the aspects of their religious traditions into a context which can prepare our youth for our unique experience of adulthood in this society.

12)   And, finally, the celebration of our youth's transition to adulthood is fun. It's an excellent reason to par-tay! Relatives may come from near and far, also former teachers, neighbors, babysitters, and mentors. Some will dance, others will sing, some will give tributes, all will eat. An appropriate celebration will model all the principles of *Orita* rites of passage and will provide hours of enjoyment, laughter and fun.

And, hopefully, all youth who participate and observe will become convinced that the passage to adulthood is wonderful, and achievable, and worth the effort - and will be strengthened to face and conquer the challenges in the years ahead.

41

Chapter 3

Mobilizing for Orita Rites of Passage

The message of this chapter is simply this: you've got exactly what it takes to generate an effective *Orita* experience for your young person.

Don't fail to get started because you can't find a sponsor or a "professional" to create a program for you. Don't be too quick to turn over the reins to others, in the mistaken belief that an expert or a "professional" or an outside organization can do a better job. Don't put it off because you think you can't afford it.

An *Orita* program is not something that's done for you, it's something you do for yourselves and for your youth. At the same time, *Orita* is neither a mass-produced nor an exclusively private undertaking. It requires the right blend of originality and communal involvement. Let's look at both sides of this formula.

You say, "how do we know you've got what it

takes?" Well, we know for a few reasons. Number one, you're here. And number two, you're reading this book. So those together indicate that you (or the youth in your life) are the descendant(s) of somebody who survived intact, despite the holocaust of the Middle Passage, slavery and / or colonialism, segregation and /or discrimination. That means, at minimum, you've got something to share with your youth. You have a legacy of a people who generated beauty out of ashes.

Furthermore, because you've been closest to your youth, you probably have a vision of what's possible for him or her. You understand something about his or her physical constitution, cultural history, intellectual and artistic capability, and maybe even spiritual calling or destiny. Your vision of a positive future for your youth is probably the most empowering gift you can give him or her. Whose view of you are you most likely to believe - the view of the persons who know you best, or that of a stranger?

An effective *Orita* program's activities and celebrations will be tailored to reflect the youth's unique needs and possibilities - and who can better make choices and judgments about the direction the program should take, than you, the persons most closely related to him or her?

So, you're the right person(s). And what does it take? *Orita* grows out of a common vision for families of African descent in America that Kwanzaa pictures in its seven days of celebration. On each day of Kwanzaa, we affirm one of these seven principles as a pillar of strong African-American communities, which contribute leaders to the world. Called Nguzo Saba in Swahili language, or Seven Principles, these constitute that vision for our communities:

Umoja
(pronounced oo-MO-jah)
Unity
Kujichagulia
(pronounced koo-jee-cha-goo-LEE-ah)
Self-determination
Ujima
(pronounced oo-JEE-mah)
Collective work and responsibility
Ujamaa
(pronounced oo-jah-MAH)
Cooperative Economics
Nia
(pronounced NEE-ah)
Purpose
Kuumba
(pronounced koo-UM-bah)
Creativity
Imani
(pronounced ee-MAH-nee)
Faith

Now, imagine yourself and your family engaging in a lifestyle that is characterized by these principles, not just during Kwanzaa, but all year long. Well, *Orita* gives you another opportunity to consciously put the principles into practice and to model them for your youth. The *Orita* experience helps develop persons who will create such communities. Consider the examples that follow:

Kujichagulia (self-determination) - how better to model that principle than that the program be organized by caring African-American adults for their own youth, youth to which they are already connected by family or community relationship.

The value of self-determination is also affirmed when we experience high quality outcomes from resources and facilities from the African-American community. At the same time, "self-reliance" need not imply that the *Orita* celebration should appear "homemade" or ordinary. On the contrary, the final ceremony and celebration should be special. They should be conducted tastefully, to a high standard of excellence, with planning comparable to that of a graduation, a Jewish bar mitzvah, a cotillion, a simple wedding, a formal ceremonial, once-in-a-lifetime affair.

Nia, Kuumba, Imani (purpose, creativity, faith) - the planning and execution of the program should demonstrate both purpose and faith, and be carried out with the unique creativity each participant brings to the project. Begin and end your meetings and activities with brief prayers for divine guidance and assistance. Keep the youth informed from the start of the project; allow them to ask questions and take their suggestions, where appropriate. Their involvement affirms our faith in them and in what God is doing in their lives, and will undoubtedly inject some youthful creativity into the overall program.

In these four principles of Kwanzaa, we see *Orita* focusing inwards: requiring self-awareness, soul-searching, personal and family commitment, spiritual motivation and divine inspiration. But, *Orita* also requires that we include the contributions of others. We argue that the village must be involved, but in a selective way. The remaining three principles characterize the role of the village.

Ujima (Collective work and responsibility) - It is important that the youth gain insight into how an important project is organized, planned, and executed. The youth will have a memorable experience, which can help prove that, contrary to stereotype, "black folks can do things right".

Umoja (unity) - among the adults generating the program unity is a key requirement, whether in the interactions of a mother and father, or an elder helping younger adults, or a group of families organizing *Orita* for several youth at once, as we did. Even where there are differences of opinion or clashes of taste, the higher purpose of celebrating our youth must be a strong enough incentive to overshadow differences among the organizers and to ensure a successful undertaking. All the rhetoric in the world won't mean a thing if youth don't experience unity as a reality among the people with whom they most closely identify.

Ujamaa (Cooperative Economics) - It's a good example for youth to see their families finance the educational program, ceremony and celebration, without going into debt. A real-life demonstration of cooperative economics, *Orita* provides an opportunity for families to share expenses, save together regularly over several months, leverage talents and skills, barter and raise funds, techniques which can ensure an affordable and first-class program. This can be achieved with good planning, even on a tight budget.

Knowing whom to ask for help
Although you've got what it takes and nobody knows your youth better than you do, the *Orita* experience will be enriched by the wisely planned involvement of others in your community. So, how do you select the right kind and degree of community support?

Having a clear vision of our own responsibility for our youth will help us know how to make wise use of the resources of others. One big decision that may challenge us is how or whether to use our affiliations with churches or other community organizations. Situations are highly variable, depending on your location, affiliations, and timing. We would caution that a lot depends on the individuals with whom you would be working in the organization. Consider the following pros and cons.

There are several benefits of having an organizational affiliation. Typically the organization has a location where activities, meetings or a celebration can be held. Organizations usually have facilities such as an auditorium, classrooms, a piano, black boards, photocopier, paper, and computers with word processing and graphics software. An organization's members can become supporters - to help make up an audience, a support network of professionals, ministers, and elders who will come and speak or work with the youth.

One of the major benefits of church or community group affiliation is credibility for the project. With an organization's backing, you are likely to get more people to participate, or to raise more funds and to lower costs.

Not every organization, however, makes a good affiliate. Consider the following checklist when seeking the backing of a church:

1) Does the church or denomination have a tradition like *Orita* in its history, which makes them comfortable with the concept?

2) Are there other youth programs in the church, whose leaders support the *Orita* program?

49

3) Do key adults and church leaders understand and value the program?

4) Are they comfortable with the Afrocentric emphasis?

5) Do they trust you to choose activities and speakers, without them censoring or unduly controlling the program?

These questions may be asked of secular organizations as well. If the answer is "no" to any of the questions, it may be best to work outside of this organizational umbrella.

Sometimes, people in your organization want to help, but have an unduly critical attitude toward young people, in general. If given the chance, such individuals enjoy 'setting kids straight', rather than building them up. A shared vision among all adults in *Orita* preparation is critical to a successful experience. Organizational affiliation must be carefully considered, and all participants should be clear what the program is and what it is not.

We believe that a most meaningful *Orita* program can be done by an individual family, an extended family, or a group of parents. After the *Orita* celebration, they may disband or continue to share joint activities.

Selecting The Village Elder

Whether your program involves a single family, a group of families or an organization, because *Orita* stresses community recognition, it is natural to expect some representative from the community to authenticate the program's outcomes. We call such an individual the "Village Elder".

If a church were involved in the program, the minister would likely play this role; however, any older person of African descent with suitable qualifications can be asked to do so. Some suggested qualifications are: someone respected in the community, preferably with graying or balding hair and having some personal knowledge of the youth, a relative, a minister, or a community professional. We advise that, if possible, the Village Elder be of the same sex as the youth or group of youth, in the program. In our *Orita* program, the "Village Elder" was a family friend who is both an ordained minister and a judge in the civil court system. He came in his robe to perform the closing ceremony and bless the youth. He also came to meet the young men at the Launch Ceremony the year before, informing them of his interest and involvement in the program and advising them that he would be following their progress and checking on them at the end of the year.

In selecting the Elder, it is important to get someone who loves youth, who is comfortable with his or her ethnicity, who has charisma and is willing to wear a traditional garb or robe and will bring humor and passion to the events they participate in. Of course, such persons must be reliable and dependable,

51

and they must be given adequate notice of the events and assure their availability.

If possible, this individual should participate in some pre-ceremony counseling of the youth. The Village Elder may be conceived of as a Wise One, an overseer, who gives the community's blessing and sanctions that the youth has satisfactorily met the *Orita* requirements. In the Appendix, we outline the full job description of this key player in the passage celebration. You should request that the recommended Village Elder read that description before finalizing his or her commitment to your program.

Parental Involvement is Key
Although the village elder is important, we believe parental involvement is even more valuable. Parents should be involved at every stage, not just at the closing ceremony or celebration. The more that parents participate in the planning the better the quality of the experience. The program can be more tailored to the specific needs and issues of the youth involved, because the parents know best what their sons and daughters struggle with. Parents know what their children's needs are; they can raise questions; they can challenge their son or daughter about what has been discussed in meetings. When parents participate, they reassure their youth that they agree with the goals of *Orita*, and, afterwards, are likely to show more respect for their son's or daughter's new status as an

adult. If youth see their parents in leadership roles, modeling the values taught during the *Orita* process, they can more readily visualize themselves growing up to assume similar roles. It may be quite a challenge to pull this off, so if you can do this, it may be a growth experience for everyone.

When we organized our program, each parent had a responsibility for either teaching a class or hosting a guest lecturer on the topic assigned to him or her. Where children had two parents, both mother and father had to take a turn being in charge. Some of the parents had college degrees or had attended college, and some had not. Some parents chose to present the topic they selected, and others invited a guest, and acted as host or hostess of the meeting. There was often visible both anxiety and pride on the faces of the youth whose parent was in charge that week. For some, it was the first time that they had ever been in a classroom, where their parent was in charge. In some cases, the youth had helped the parent prepare or distribute handouts; the son often had the first question or comment in the discussion part of the presentation.

When guest speakers were invited, they were usually "ordinary" people, mostly men, since ours was a program for young men, invited for their experience, insight, testimonies, and ability to relate well with young men. The point is you don't need the political clout and deep pockets to attract celebrities to speak to your youth. There are men and women, near you and from far away, who will gladly donate their time, and who can add to your own contributions to help create a rich *Orita* experience for your youth.

You can afford it!
You don't have to go broke to finance an unforgettable and joyous *Orita* celebration. It should cost some time, effort, and money, but only in proportion to your resources.

Time
The popular African proverb, "it takes a whole village to raise a child", implies a community sharing responsibility for its children. In traditional cultures, the costs in time, effort and money to rear youth are viewed as a communal obligation, the nuclear family alone being inadequate to provide all of the experiences required to bring a youth to successful adulthood. The community has a vested interest in ensuring that its values are perpetuated in the next generation, for the survival and progress of the entire culture.

It will certainly be appropriate to ask individuals to donate their time, by coming out to speak to or to work with your youth during the educational component. People will be more inclined to help the more they see parents making sacrifices and investing seriously in the process.

54

Everyone who participates in the closing ceremony should rehearse or do some pre-work to ensure the quality and timing of their contribution. The idea is to provide our youth a memory of an outstanding experience that they and the significant people in their lives prepared and executed, an important memory that will sustain them in times of uncertainty later in life.

If the *Orita* program is led by community or church professionals, parents will be expected to spend time monitoring the educational program, reviewing with son or daughter the topics discussed and information learned, and helping him or her rehearse the closing speech or memory work in Scripture or black history. If parents are leading the program, time will be required to attend meetings, to seek out quality experiences, and to find good materials. All of this can be challenging, especially for single parents or families where both parents work, or are in school themselves.

Dedicating time is another reason why parents (or others who will work with the youth) must think well in advance about their son's or daughter's rites of passage. If *Orita* is going to be observed in his or her 13th year, then when the child is 10 or 11 years old, and even in early childhood, parents should start thinking about what kinds of experiences they want to create for the passage year. Jotting down ideas, networking, and making contacts, advising friends and relatives that passage time is near and what your hopes are for their involvement will ensure availability of more resources when your *Orita* is finally underway. Think about relatives out-of-town or friends who live in the country, people whom you would like your child to get to know or to meet, but with whom you rarely converse or visit. Is there an elderly black person, over 65 years of age, who is in good health and who can spend time with your son or daughter, telling them about how life was for black people when they were young? Start early to arrange a trip to see these folk, or to determine whether one of them is travelling into your area soon. Write about *Orita* in letters, holiday greetings, or a family newsletter. Line up experiences and activities, so that when that year comes, you will already have a kit full of ideas ready to be implemented, whether for one or a group of youth. The more special experiences your son or daughter comes to associate with his or her rites of passage year, the more memorable the whole process will be.

What has been said here about parents will not be realistic for every family. That depends on health, educational level, work and financial situation, proximity to their hometown, and a host of other factors, which may vary from year to year. In any event, the experience will be richer for the youth if it is shared either with other youth of the same age, or with other adults of African descent, who are outside the circle of friends of his or her own parents.

Effort

Although long-term thinking and planning will reduce the intensity of the effort which *Orita* requires, when the program is over, it should be clear, both to our youth and to the community, that we believe our youth are worth the great amount of effort that will have been expended.

Keeping in mind that we've estimated the scale of the *Orita* ceremony and celebration as midway between the average birthday party and an elaborate wedding, *Orita* should involve more planning and effort than the former but far less extravagance than the latter. It would not be unreasonable to expect some relatives who live out-of-town to attend the closing ceremony, as a sign of support. For the ceremony and celebration, most participants will have taken time off from other work, worn special clothing, prepared speeches and prayers or performed music, dance, poetry, or oratory, and some will have created contributions by cooking, weaving, painting, or otherwise crafting handmade gifts.

For the preparation component of the rites of passage program, some members of the community will have taken part in some aspect of the course of study and practice. For the physical challenge of our son's *Orita* program, some men who were not fathers of the young men, traveled and assisted in the somewhat grueling mountain-climbing experience. Some presenters at the preparation classes invested considerable effort in preparing materials and activities that would ensure an effective learning experience for the youth.

For the persons who will organize the program, successful planning will entail timely completion of numerous tasks—from telephoning, to hosting meetings and arranging events, to cleaning up after events and sending thank-you notes. A primer on managing projects is included in the next chapter, to help you keep track of such details. By appropriately setting the scale of the program, you can generate a quality *Orita* program that incorporates the level of effort and the amount of help you can enlist to make it happen. Whatever scope you decide on, give it all you've got and your youth will be the better for it.

Money

There are three major areas where money emerges as a factor in *Orita*: gift-giving, funding and spending.

Gift-giving: For the celebration, friends may bring gifts for the youth, but this is not essential and the youth should not focus on gifts as a major motivation for participating. To the extent that there are gifts, the emphasis should be on value - things that are handmade, things that are customized, things that are contributed; these things are valuable because they represent people's time, talent, and sacrifice. And we all know that the most valuable things are not usually those that money can buy. At the same time, because our culture tends to evaluate things by how much money is spent on them, we want to exhibit some level of saving, spending, and monetary contribution time, which will underscore how important the program is to us.

In most *Orita* programs that we know of, at the closing ceremony, the parents have presented a relatively costly gift to their youth. The idea is that the gift is durable enough to be passed on to the youth's offspring in years to come. In two cases we know, a gold medallion engraved with *Orita* insignia was custom made and presented to the youths to treasure and to be passed on to a descendant at a future *Orita* celebration. In our program, we collectively purchased kente cloth strips, a $50 savings bond and a New Testament for each youth, with the kente strip to be passed on for future generations.

Funding: Participating family members should agree on how you want to fund your *Orita*, and then decide on a level of spending that matches the resources of the funding sources. Remember that the money spent on the entire program should neither exceed the resources of the participants, nor come exclusively from one source. *Orita* should provide a life lesson in using what is available as well as what is possible through creativity, faith and communal effort.

The way you fund the project should model the Seven Principles. We think the ideal is that the youth themselves, their parents and other organizers invest money, perhaps over several weeks or months. Unsolicited and solicited donations from others may supplement, but should not outweigh, family investment.

One approach to funding might be to review your family yearly income and determine a percentage that seems a reasonable investment in your child. Many families spend 25 percent of gross income on their mortgage note or rent. Some families tithe or give 10 percent of income to their church or charities. Some spend that percentage or more every year on private or parochial school education that does not always reflect the family's values. Would a one-time expenditure of one percent of your combined annual family income be an unreasonable investment in your son or daughter's transition to adulthood? For a quick estimate, drop the last two digits of your salary and see what you get. $250? $300? $500? $800? or more. For many, this would be the cost of a new wardrobe, a summer vacation or day camp, babysitting for a few weeks/ months, depending on where you live.

If a group of families get together, each contributing over the course of a year a total of a few hundred dollars, they can both keep individual family contributions low as well as take advantage of quantity pricing. In this way, they can come up with something more elaborate or elegant than each family might have been able to afford acting alone. You can usually negotiate a cheaper unit cost, for such items as food or printing, when you buy for a larger number of persons. Also, there will be some families who earn more than the others do, some with two or more incomes and others with one or none. Some may be willing to help make up for a shortfall of another family. A word of caution here, however. It is not advisable for any one or two families to dominate the event - either by contributing much more than the others, or by participating more in the ceremony, or by having more relatives and well wishers than the others. We recommend that the group plan on a scale that's reasonable even for the family with a single parent, or unemployed parent or parent on public assistance, to make a significant contribution. One way to do this is to encourage all the families to do personal fund-raising to make their share; none of the others needs to know whether their contribution came from income or donations.

We had quite a range of financial ability in our group, some whose combined family income was in the six-figure range, and others with more modest earnings, struggling with chronic underemployment. Some parents had graduate degrees; others may have lacked a high school diploma. Each family agreed to contribute $300, and we actually collected more than that amount, for a total of just under $2,500. The passage of seven young men was celebrated for a cash outlay of $2,800, with the difference made up in contributions. Some of the families who had trouble coming up with their $300 got help from their relatives and friends.

A final funding consideration: some parents in our group suggested that we approach political representatives for government funds. While this is a community event, it is not something that we should expect government agencies to underwrite. In whatever political era we have lived, whether during the dominance of "big government" liberals or "states rights" conservatives, we have never been able to expect our local or larger governments to provide African-American youth the kind of support a rites of passage requires. That situation is not likely to change as we enter the twenty-first century, where there are larger ethnic "minorities" than we are, and when even "whites" may become a minority.

Spending: In the next chapter, we will walk you through developing the budget for *Orita*. By following the disciplined planning process described there, you will encounter few unexpected expenses, and the level of your spending for the project will not significantly exceed the amount budgeted. Going into debt should be avoided at all costs, if you are to effectively model our Kwanzaa principles for your youth. And, consider including your youth in some discussions about funding the program. They should understand what the level of spending is and should be shown that the spending was consistent with the amount of funding.

Whatever the budget, whether for a group or for a single youth, a memorable and elegant occasion which honors the youth's accomplishment and which demonstrates the collective talent and caring of his family and friends, can be achieved at a price that's affordable to all involved. Remember that money doesn't buy what really counts. What really counts here is the quality of the relationships that develop, the experiences that the youth have, the people they get to know, the things they learn.

In the end, we felt that we had not been able to provide as rich an experience for our youth as we would have liked to, but lack of money was not the primary reason. If we had done more consistent and better planning, several ideas that we had hoped to implement might have been realized. For example, one of the things that we had hoped to do was to organize mentoring or apprenticeship experiences with older black men, who have special skills or information. While it would have cost almost no money to implement, it would have been an enriching experience for our youth, many of whom have no living grandparents or extended family to draw on for such opportunities. Our failure to realize this goal was a result of inadequate planning and follow-up, not lack of funds.

Rather than worrying that we may not be able to afford a rites-of-passage project, the bigger question is, "Can we afford not to do this?" What does it cost when our youth lose their way? There's no guarantee that a rites of passage program will safeguard our youth from failure and disappointment. But, for far less time and money than it would take to extricate them from the criminal justice system or an addiction or emotional distress, we can provide a memory, at the very least, that can jolt them into reality at some future point in their lives when things are rather low. At best, a rites of passage program can become a seminal experience that will actually turn our youth's life around.

How to know if you're doing a good job
If each family or group can tailor its *Orita* program in so many ways, how can you be sure that you're doing it right? Well, we believe that, initially, most people who go to the trouble of organizing an *Orita* program have the kind of concern and intelligence to do a wonderful job.

The following checklist to assess the health of your program may be helpful:
1) Do the youth meet on time, with 100% attendance, prepared with completed homework assignments?
2) Do the youth ask questions, actively engage in discussions, showing respect for and listening to one another?

3) Are the adult participants (organizers, mentors, speakers, supporters) carrying out their commitments? 4) Are there aspects of the program which focus on spiritual, intellectual, economic and community issues? 5) Is the plan on schedule for celebrating the end of the youth's transition year? 6) Do you have a good feeling that God and your foreparents would be proud of what's going on in the program?

If you can answer "yes" to these questions, then your program is probably a winner. If you have to answer "no" to any, then identify and resolve the problems. Don't give up.

We want to see the *Orita* tradition survive and expand. It has to be adaptable for parents and organizers at every level of African-American society, from the rich and famous to the ordinary and poor. The highly educated and the uneducated, the rural, suburban and urban families must all be able to involve their youth in such an experience. It has taken about 30 years for the annual Kwanzaa observance to become widely recognized and practiced among African-Americans. In a similar way, we hope *Orita* will grow to be a family tradition for as long as there are children of African descent living in America.

Whichever approach you decide on, your child has a God-ordained destiny to achieve what no other person can. The *Orita* rites of passage is not targeted for the problem child, it's for every child of African descent, to realize his or her special purpose in life. Get started today.

Chapter 4:

Planning your *Orita* project

Planning your *Orita* Program involves five basic steps that, when followed, will ensure that you have accomplished what you set out to do.

1. Your Vision
Write down a vision for your youth as an adult. This involves visualizing your youth in five, ten or more years and describing his or her strengths, character, skills, capabilities, associates and other attributes. Mark those items in your vision that the *Orita* process can help develop. For example, you may note that, as a result of participating in the program, your youth will be more self-confident, assertive, studious,

67

more highly developed in some character trait, or will have made a significant contribution to society.

2. Your Strategies

Create strategies that will allow you to realize your vision. For example, a strategy for achieving assertiveness might be to require each participant to write and deliver a speech before an audience, during the *Orita* closing ceremony. Another strategy for achieving self-confidence might be to require each participant to take part in a physical challenge (long hike up a mountain, or other athletic test). In addition to specific strategies for your youth, some overall program strategies need to be established at this step. These include deciding how you will fund the project and which other youth, if any will share in this *Orita* program. Will there be other youth? Will the others be all boys, all girls, or boys and girls? What will their ages be?

3. The Tasks

Once the strategies are in place, develop the actual tasks required to carry out the strategies and complete the program becomes step three. For example, scheduling events, gathering needed materials and resources, and assigning responsibilities to specific individuals are just a few of the tasks required. We used checklists and a scheduling chart to identify all the tasks, schedules and assignments.

4. Doing It

Execute and monitor all the tasks, through project completion. Follow-up planning meetings, reminder notes, and schedule adjustments are an essential part of making sure that things just get done as planned, even if some unforeseen circumstances arise.

5. The Finish

Carry out activities that are required to bring closure to the process. These range from paying outstanding bills to writing thank you notes and a financial report.

None of these steps should be a big deal! In fact, knowing where you are going, how you're going to get there, and then developing a good plan and carrying it out to completion, is a formula for success and enjoyment for the organizers of any project.

So, now the fun begins. We start to work on each of these steps. From now to the end of this book, we will be creating an *Orita* program that works. We will make visions and plans, for this our first *Orita*. If you don't have any original ideas for your program, don't worry. You can use ours.

First, write down your vision. Make a copy of the *Orita* Vision Worksheet in in Figures 4-1A, B. Start by writing your name on the first line, and leaving room for the names of others who will help you plan.

Create A Vision

When our group shared our individual visions for our sons, the following profile emerged:
- he is assertive
- he has excellent character
- he practices practical Christianity
- he has learned that he must pass on his religious faith
- he understands his ethnic heritage
- he is a disciplined thinker
- he is self-aware, and aware of his goals
- he has developed close and lasting friendships with peers who share similar values
- he is physically fit
- he knows right from wrong
- he can stand up before an audience and speak articulately
- he understands that sexuality alone doesn't make a man
- he handles his own and other people's money wisely

Our vision list grew out of brainstorming, having everyone answer questions like, "what would I like to see my son being, or doing, in five years? in ten years?" What is going on in society / my community that I don't want for my son?

You may not have a group of parents who shareyour values or vision for youth. You may be only a couple, like Paul and Jeanne McKean, who started discussing their vision when their children were

8 and 10 years old. Their work ended up in a book entitled *Leading a Child to Independence*, in which the authors described a systematic approach to preparing their children for successful passage through adolescence. They had developed the program by trial and error and study of the Scriptures, starting by discussing their views about parenting with each other even before getting married, and continuing by dedicating weekends to planning as their children grew.

"We began", Paul McKean said, "by asking ourselves some questions: 'What do we want our children to be like when they are eighteen and on their own? How will they conduct themselves when we are not around? How will they handle tough issues without our input?'"

The McKeans assessed their children's strengths and weaknesses - spiritually, emotionally, physically, intellectually, socially, and financially. Then they set specific goals in these areas and formed a vision of their children at age18. When their children were safely through adolescence, they put their plan into book form, along with worksheets in each area to share their insights with other parents.

You may have thought a lot about what your children may be like in the future. If you have not written down that vision, now is the time to evaluate your child and create a vision of who you want him or her to be at the end of adolescence. According to Dr. Stephen Covey, popular management guru, the first of the "Seven Habits of Highly Effective People" is to "start with the end in view." Effective parents do not drift through their children's early years without having a vision for their child when he or she is ready to leave the nest. Your vision will guide you in selecting the right strategies for your child's passage experience.

Identify and select specific strategies
Based on your vision for your youth, identify and select specific strategies, which you will implement during the *Orita* project. For example, one key *Orita* requirement is to have your youth prepare and effectively deliver an autobiographical speech of a few hundred words, before the audience at the closing ceremony. If your vision is that your youth will be an articulate public speaker as a young adult, demonstrating these skills makes sense for a passage program.

Another strategy which will be commonly included in *Orita* programs is to have each youth successfully complete an experience which is physically and emotionally challenging, such as a wilderness experience, a rigorous mountain climb, or other outdoor adventure. This challenging requirement supports the vision of a young adult committed to physical fitness.

In our program, we selected certain information, which we believed our youth should know thoroughly. Early in the *Orita* year, our youth knew that they would be asked to recite by heart at the closing ceremony the first and last names of all known grandparents and great-grandparents, on both sides of their family. We expected them to know the 7 Principles of Kwanzaa in Swahili and in English. We chose the Apostles' Creed, the Lord's Prayer, the Beatitudes, and the names of the books of the Bible as scriptural information for our youth to commit to memory. Each of these items matched some part of our vision, for example, awareness of self, understanding their ethnic heritage, knowing right from wrong, and passing on their religious faith.

You can draw on this book and other resources for help in identifying appropriate strategies for achieving your vision. As you read this chapter, mark those ideas that best address your concerns. Share your ideas with others. Attend rites of passage ceremonies of other young people in your community. Identify other youth in your child's age group, who would benefit from such a program. Mobilize their parents or other caregivers to come on board.

Once you've organized a core group of planners, lots of conversations should take place among yourselves. Because several families were involved in our project, we met at different homes to share our vision and to discuss possible *Orita* strategies. What were some of the areas in which we needed help to round out our son's preparation for adulthood? As

73

different ones shared, someone took notes, and together the group arrived at common emphases that all could agree on. Whatever required growth was an area for the program to address. Note next to each strategy the part of the vision that the strategy supports. Involve the young people, at some point in these discussions. Assure them that you have a vision and a program, but invite their feedback and answer their questions, to gain some insight and their buy-in as early as possible in the planning. Twelve year olds, and certainly, older teenagers, can make very significant input. We had each of our sons draw pictures of what his life would look like in five years and in ten years. We encouraged them to show specifics: clothing, work, residence, and lifestyle. These drawings generated conversation and gave us insights into what aspects of adult life were on their minds, and about what kinds of questions might motivate them to focus on future goals.

General strategies
There are several strategic questions that must be answered during this "Strategies" phase. Our group found that we had to engage in some pretty frank discussion in order to resolve these. We mention them here, because they are likely to come up for others. Should we include youth of both sexes in the program? Should a sibling of the opposite sex partici-

pate in any of the sessions of a single sex program? Should siblings of the same sex but of different ages go through the passage together? We recommend that you consider the following in answering such questions. Will the program be able to effectively focus on the needs of each participating youth, ensuring that he or she achieves the goals and is ready for passage to adulthood? The more specific the target population, the more the youths have in common, the more specific the training can be, and the more successful you are likely to be. If the scope of the endeavor is too broad, you will not be very effective.

On the other hand, you may be able to benefit from the involvement of certain other youth and their families, and this consideration should be weighed against the benefits of a more narrow focus. So, for example, we prefer that an *Orita* program involve at least two or more youth, rather than a single boy or girl. We also recommend single sex programs, and for youth of the same age, or within at most a year or two's age difference. This may mean having multiple programs to accommodate all the youth involved. Multiple *Orita* programs should be happening every year in any family or community of families of African descent, since most likely some youths are making their passages to adulthood every year.

We prefer to see each sibling participate in his or her own passage celebration. In this way, each can have his or her opportunity to be challenged fully and to gain recognition for having moved through the passage successfully. Sometimes there are very subtle, even unconscious issues between siblings, which may not surface when most of their activities are done in concert. The opportunity for significant achievement that is clearly attributed to one, without the other sibling, may be very important in the personal development of the participant.

If this is a group program, there should be a small enough number of youth, so that each can participate fully, be observed closely and be encouraged and counseled, as needed. Each youth should have an opportunity to make a major speech at the closing celebration; a large group of 10 or more would make individual speeches impractical.

While selecting strategies, the planners should know exactly who the participants will be. Is it for one youth? Is it for a group of youth? Should it be for youth in puberty (around age 12 - 13), or for older teenagers, say age 15 or 16? How important is individual achievement, or are group presentations more desirable?

It may take a while to narrow down your lists of possible *Orita* strategies to arrive at a coherent approach to the project. In future years, when *Orita* has been established as a tradition in the African-American community, certain components will become ritualized. People will have common concepts of why a rites of passage program is done. Until then, families may need to visit programs or read a book, to get a clear and consistent picture. Before our first meeting, we had circulated copies of Rev. Frank Fair's book, whose name and graphic symbol we used as well. Unfortunately, this excellent reference work was not in print at the time of this writing.

Having your youth attend other youth's rites of passage programs will plant the seeds of acceptance and anticipation in their minds. Until rites of passage is widely practiced in American culture; parents will have to allow time for your child to accept the idea. Ultimately, if your child is adamant that he or she does not wish to participate in such a process, it is not advisable to force it upon him or her. One of your critical tasks will be to fully engage your youth in participating in and contributing to the *Orita* experience, and wanting to pass on the tradition to his or her children in the future.

Financial strategies
In the last chapter, in the section titled "You Can Afford It", we identified three key areas that may be considered strategic: gift giving, funding, and spending. You may want to review that material with the other planners and then agree on a target dollar amount for the project. Next, compare the strategies you have selected for the program with that figure. Some strategies may be eliminated at this point. After that, any

gaps will have to be made up by a funding strategy, which may include saving, selling, or soliciting donations of money, material or services.

It may be that you will decide that not everyone is going to be able to afford the same level of contribution. Perhaps those who can afford more will help to cover those who can't; or you may decide to plan the celebration to accommodate the lowest common denominator that all the families can comfortably afford, so no one feels that they're getting charity. But, at the end, people have to be frank, honest. You should do whatever seems right. Whatever it takes to get the job done.

In our planning, some families wanted us to seek outside funding, say by a black community organization. That may work in some situations. In the end, we decided to do it with our own funds, to open a bank account and save all year before the celebration. We deposited money into the bank account anonymously - each family got deposit slips, which could be submitted at a variety of bank branches around the city. We decided that our budget would not exceed $3000. and every family was expected to come up with at least $300. over the course of a year. If we found that our account didn't make the target, we'd find a way to raise the difference. Some people decided to ask their guests at the celebration to pay admission; others decided to pay to cover their guests. A fund-raising letter was written, and families signed and mailed it to whomever they wished, at their discretion. Others preferred not to solicit funds. Parents and leaders should try to talk very openly, at a gut level, about their goals, needs, and concerns. The atmosphere should be open and non-threatening; distractions should be minimal, so people can really share. Pray with the other planners, and with the youth, and seek God's blessing on every stage of the planning and execution.

Plan Tasks

After you have clarified your vision and identified your strategies, the goal of the next phase of planning is to arrive at a detailed and structured list of activities and tasks which can be completed in the timeframe available, and by the people whose names will be assigned to them. You will find it easier to arrive at this goal if you follow a step-by-step procedure, which can be remembered by asking key questions about each idea or suggestion, The questions are: what? how? who? when? The trick is not to ask the questions when the ideas come up. Too many questions at the start tend to stifle people's ideas. Rather, limit your first round of questions to simply answering "what?" for all the ideas. Then, on a second round, answer "how?" for all. Then "who?" and so on.

What?

At the beginning of this phase, don't be too quick to

ORITA VISION WORKSHEET

Name(s) of *Orita* program
planner(s):_____

VISION OF THE YOUTH AS AN ADULT:

(1)   Spiritual Life

_____

_____

(2)   Character

_____

_____

(3)   Knowledge

_____

_____

(4)   Emotional Life

_____

_____

(5)   Physical

_____

_____

(6)   Other

_____

Figure 4-1A

```
┌─────────────────────────────────────────────────┐
│  STRATEGIES FOR REALIZING THE VISION:           │
│      Specific Strategies:                        │
│                                                  │
│      Consider: skills development, physical tests,│
│  community involvement, travel, knowledge, finances, arts, │
│  afrocentricity, scriptures.                     │
│                                                  │
│  Vision                                          │
│   #___   _____       │
│   #___   _____       │
│   #___   _____       │
│   #___   _____       │
│   #___   _____       │
│   #___   _____       │
│          General Strategies:                     │
│              Number of youth _____       │
│              Single-sex or joint_____      │
│              Age range _____      │
│              Sponsors? _____      │
│              Target spending level: $_____     │
│              Funding sources:                    │
│              each family contribution? $_____    │
│              donations of services?_____      │
│              other donations?_____      │
│              charge fees? for _____      │
│              sell? _____      │
│              solicitations? from _____      │
└─────────────────────────────────────────────────┘
```

Figure 4-1B

rule out ideas; at least consider creative or wacky-sounding ideas as you brainstorm specific features of your *Orita* program. Use nouns, if at all possible. Jot them down on yellow self-sticking notes or index cards; bad ones can be eliminated later. Some good sources for ideas are holes in your youth's development - things they are not learning in school; things

81

they are not learning in church; things we don't get to do enough at home; places we don't get to go; things they will need if they are to be well rounded.

When we brainstormed our list of features and activities, the nouns we came up with appear as randomly as we wrote them down in the box in Figure 4-2.

We then rearranged the list of nouns into logical groups under the headings of *Orita* program components:

Figure 4-2

- things that have to do with the study components (academic, social, spiritual)
- things that have to do with the closing ceremony
- things that have to do with the closing celebration
- things that are essential for the planners to stay in touch and achieve the vision

Figure 4-3 shows how we matched the words to phases of an *Orita* program. Now's the time to weed out any ideas either that don't fit the vision or on which your group can't agree. Finally, organize an outline with each major

Related Ideas	Orita Component
Music, band, poems, songs, dinner, catering hall, special outfits, church basement, Roots - Kunta Kinte, African attire, kente cloth, youth of the opposite sex	CELEBRATION
Elder, minister, prayers, blessings, speakers, speeches	CEREMONY
Novels by authors of African descent, Bible verses, church creeds, family tree, black history museum, Bible study	STUDY
Trips, obstacle course, physical challenge, picnic, tee shirts, wilderness experience, fasting	STUDY
Savings / dues, fund raising, bank account, committees, officers	PLAN

Figure 4-3

Orita component followed by detailed tasks. This outline captures the main aspects of the project at a glance, and allows everyone to conceive of everything that has to be done in a simple and manageable way.

How?

To make this a task-oriented phase, you'll have to convert these nouns into action items. Your next step is to attach verbs to the nouns. "HOW do we take action on these WHAT items?" What *actions* need to be taken?

"Bank account" becomes "open an account at First National, so we can deposit funds all year." "Administration" becomes "select a corresponding secretary and a treasurer." "Physical challenge" becomes "take the youth on a wilderness retreat." "Music" becomes "hire a band for the celebration." "Black books" becomes "assign each youth to read three novels by black authors."

At the same time, we want to refer back to our vision worksheet to make sure that we are not going away from our original strategies. Later on we may decide to change the strategies, maybe to accommodate a youth with a special need or situation. In planning the program for our son, one of our strategies did change somewhat, after we began to plan, in order to include a couple of other families, whose sons didn't quite fit our original age group. It is important to the continued success of the planning, however, that all agree to any changes in strategy, just as you needed to agree on your original ones. Even if the plan changes a lot, as long as it remains consistent with the vision of the participants, everyone will become more and more enthusiastic and work harder as success comes closer to being a reality.

Who?

After we have itemized the tasks we need to do, we must assign ourselves or others to perform them. A review of chapter 3 ("Mobilizing for *Orita* Rites of Passage") may be helpful in this planning phase.

Next to each task in the task outline, a name should be written, at least tentatively assigning who's going to be responsible for either doing the task or for finding the right person to do it. For example, in planning the Study component of our program, we determined that we would have about 15 sessions to cover the topics we wanted. We knew we would need a certain number of presenters or facilitators, and each family had to be responsible for planning 1 - 3 sessions and to either invite speakers or to research the topic to present it themselves.

List all the available resources — primarily depending on the parents involved, but also considering well-wishers, relatives, friends, neighbors, ministers, grandparents and godparents, schoolteachers, and Sunday School teachers —all the people you think will help. Some of them will not help. Some may actually turn you down flat. And, there may be other people who will hear about what you're doing, and who will volunteer or ask to be invited, whom you would never have thought of, but are excited about the idea and want to help. But, you make a list of resources, and you keep it up to date.

How Much?

A crucial aspect of the "Task planning" phase is estimating how much you expect it will cost to carry out each task. At the end of this step of planning, you will be closer to having a detailed budget and to deciding exactly where to seek donations.

Once the families have agreed on a target dollar amount, major decisions can be made, even in advance. Such decisions are whether or not you will hire a caterer for the celebration; whether you're going to rent your classroom and meeting space; whether or not you will include an overnight or out-of-town trip in the Study component; what kinds of speakers you will have; how elaborate the gifts are that you will present to the youth at the ceremony; whether you can afford a videographer, professional photographer, or a musical group?

When we organized our *Orita* program, we had several conversations about whether or not to ask participants and supporters to contribute to costs of the program. For us, the most costly expense of our celebration was the cost of catering by a community-based restaurant. Some parents wanted to ask attendees at the closing event to contribute a donation to help defray the cost of the meal. Others felt strongly that our supporters should be "treated" to a meal. Because we had differing and strong opinions on the subject, we decided not to print on the invitations any reference to a fee, but to allow individual parents the freedom to ask their family and friends for donations for the meal.

Many items and services provided for the *Orita* celebration may be donated. Set standards, however, to ensure that quality and reliability aren't jeopardized in the effort to save money. Consider the following areas for donations:

• For the closing ceremony, you may find amateur photographers, videographers, caterers, and musicians, who offer to donate their services. Ask for the names of others for whom they've done work and contact those references. Ask to see samples of their work or to attend an upcoming event they'll be servicing. If you depend on them and their work turns out to be of poor quality, a key feature of your celebration may be ruined.

• Donations of food and transportation for special events, provided by well wishers and parents, may be very helpful. For example, at the beginning of the Study component, we held a launching ceremony in a public park, followed by a picnic. The elder who would preside at our closing a year later came to speak to the youth, advising them of his commitment and promising to check on them as the year progressed. During the year, when seasons permitted, we had other picnics and gatherings, to encourage the youth (and parents) to get to know each other, to work together, and to forge friendships that they could draw on in adulthood. Refreshments for these events were all donated by the participating families, each one bringing a dish or other item. Perhaps someone has access to a van or bus to take the youth on a trip or other outing.

• Facilities can be donated—rooms to hold meetings, spaces for gatherings, facilities for the closing event. Again, quality should not be sacrificed unnecessarily to keep costs down. Usually a church or community center will donate such space, or rent it at low cost or for a voluntary donation.

• Speakers and workshop leaders will often donate their services. You want to try to find those who will come without charging a fee, or who will accept a token gift to cover transportation or materials expenses, only.

• Lesson materials for the youth, books, educational materials, photocopies of homemade materials were all donated by parents in our group throughout the year-long *Orita* Study component.

• We made for the youth custom T-shirts, engraved with the symbol of the *Orita* rites of passage program, *Orita*, which we adapted from Rev. Fair's book. The artwork and shirts were donated by one of the parents in our group, who was trained in graphic design.

At the end of this chapter, we have included a sample list of items in the budget. After identifying those goods and services that you are pretty sure you can obtain for "free", you can finalize your budget and make an expense schedule. Show the amounts that have to be paid by certain times (such as a deposit for the caterer), and try to make sure there is enough cash in the account to cover the expense. Don't forget miscellaneous costs like postage, trip admission fees, and refreshments, which can add up.

When? Depending On What? And Where?

Perhaps the most critical aspect of managing any project is scheduling and controlling time. It has been said that a goal isn't really a goal until it has a time and place attached to it. Dates should be assigned to the tasks and adjusted as participants confirm their availability.

In scheduling, it may become apparent that you have not allowed adequate time. We believe that, if possible, a year is an ideal timeframe for carrying out an *Orita* project. A year provides an extended period of time, to build commitment among the parents and youth, to get commitments from others who will participate, to reserve space for classes, trips, events, and the celebration. It allows time for vacations and other social commitments, for cancellations and changes in the planned schedule, to take advantage of various seasons of the year. If you allow yourself a year, it's the kind of level of preparation that's often given to a graduation, a wedding, a cotillion - it adds seriousness of purpose to the project in the eyes of the youth. It allows even for those hard-to-get, always busy people to plan to attend and/or participate. Over the course of a year, you can take advantage of seasonal bargains.

Once you have organized the activities logically, it becomes easier to figure out how to organize the work effort, and which skills will be needed. Tasks that require more time, and those that have to be done in sequence, are the bases for developing a timetable.

In project management jargon, related tasks, which must be done in sequence, have "dependencies". What activities can't be done until certain other things are in place? Which activities have to be completed at the same time?

Expect your first plans for dates and times to be changed several times. Be sure that the locations you plan to use are available at the times you need them. Even after you have begun your program, you may find it necessary to change facilities and times, to safeguard your standards and goals. An example, in planning our Study component, was the matter of where we would hold the classes. At first, because our families lived an average of fifteen miles apart, we thought we would have meetings and classes in the various homes of the families, or at one home, which was centrally located. Classes were set for 6:30 on alternate Saturday evenings. Instead, we found families routinely arriving late and classes not getting started until around 8. After arriving late, the evening was shot, so people stayed late. So, our classes turned into all-evening, social events.

To help keep our focus and be more disciplined, we decided to "rent" a facility for the classes / meetings. We were fortunate to find a local cultural center, where music and dance lessons were given on Saturdays, and which stayed open until 7:30 PM. They were willing to rent us a classroom for 2 hours during the less busy hours on Saturdays, until closing time, for the nominal charge of $10. per hour. So for $20 or $25 per meeting, (about $3 per family per meeting), we paid to be forced to start and end on time, and to give everyone the benefit of several hours afterward to shop or cook or go out or get ready for church. It worked! A similar kind of arrangement might work for Friday evenings, or Saturday mornings, or any other time that's good for the families and youth involved.

Once the critical matter of space for gatherings and events is resolved, families can finalize that they can participate in the project or not. If you're renting space from an organization, try to get their calendar for the year. From there, you can set up your schedule—you'll know how often you can meet there, you can avoid dates where they are heavily committed. The space may be available, but a noisy wedding or band concert may effectively make your speaker or even other participants in a discussion inaudible. Among the families, parents should bring their personal planners/calendars to the planning meeting. It's amazing how many annual or prior commitments busy families can have—especially if they are active in different church and community activities. Try to pick out the month in the next year when the closing celebration will be held. If it's a busy month like June, be aware of the potential for conflicts with weddings and graduations. We originally planned for May, but at the end, wound up having our celebration very early in June.

Once you have a pretty good idea of who will be a resource and what their availability is, you can put several schedules together. There are schedules of meetings, schedules of classes, schedules of trips; you'll need to research places for the celebration— how much it will cost to use the place, what hours of the day they'll be available, what dates are still open next year, etc.

Other design tasks have to do with administration. You need to delegate someone to handle the money, open a bank account and report on the finances of the group. You need someone to take care of communications—stamps, reminders of meetings, telephone calls, mailing lists, notifications of cancellations and reschedulings, postcards.

In any sizeable project, there will be several tracks on which things are going on at the same time. There is planning for the celebration, planning for the meetings, and the infrastructure—meetings, finances, awards, etc. The more people who are involved and take responsibility for different aspects of the planning, the better the level of commitment and the more creative ideas will come in. If at all possible, try to avoid this being the brainchild of one individual or family - and, although inevitably, some will have a higher level of commitment than others, the more it is a collective effort, the more instructive and memorable this will be for the youth involved.

Doing It
Once the design and plan is in place, the third project management phase is execution or implementation. Work your plan. Manage changes. Stay on course.

The implementation phase involves a lot of scheduling and rescheduling, meeting cancellations due to weather and unanticipated events, someone has to be enough of a leader or decision maker to arrange make up sessions or to reschedule or arrange swaps of dates. There will be bad weather. Make the adjustments and make sure you stay on course. There may need to be times of recreation in between, there may be misunderstandings or problems among the youth, which have to be addressed in a special session or with a special activity. There need to be times of fun.

Some risk management should be included in planning. Allow for contingencies; backups for people who fail to arrive, extra rehearsals, extra time, extra money, extra food, and extra equipment.

The important part of the implementation phase is making sure that you are moving closer to our goals, and that critical steps are taken before the closing program. The closing program is going to reflect the activities that actually took place during implementation. Although the closing program should be designed early enough to allow adequate rehearsals, it cannot be complete until all the key activities and learning objectives have taken place—and can be celebrated.

Finish It
A good finish to a project is important in ensuring that people want to see a similar project happen again. This is particularly true of *Orita*, since we are building a tradition that we want others to carry on. The ceremony and celebration bring the process to a joy-

ful conclusion. Afterwards, participants should be shown appreciation through appropriate expressions of thanks. Bills should be paid promptly. The organizing committee should meet to discuss what went right and what might need to be repaired. Lessons learned should be written down, and passed on to other parents or for planning for other siblings in the family.

We close this chapter with a project plan chart that shows key tasks we completed to make our *Orita* project successful. Although no two *Orita* processes are exactly the same, because our youth are different, the chart provides an overview of the work required to bring our program to fruition.

ORITA PROJECT

Program Planning
- Vision / kickoff meeting
- **monthly planning meetings**
- select corresponding secretary
- open & manage bank account & funds

Project Launch
- select / confirm Village Elder
- select / confirm launch ceremony date
- **Launch event planning**
  - design / produce Tee shirts
  - assemble study notebooks
  - organize opening picnic
  - organize launch ceremony
  - plan contingency location
  - arrange for photographer
- Launch celebration

Study Component
- **Study component planning**
  - determine curriculum
  - reserve rooms / schedule classes
  - obtain materials, books, copies
  - organize / implement sou-sou
  - organize trips / special events
  - organize study days
- **Classes**
- review / evaluate youth portfolios
- conduct physical challenge
- conclude study component

Closing Ceremony
- **Invitations**
  - Design / print invitations
  - Mail invitations / collect RSVPs
- plan / write ceremony
- secure ceremony participants
- secure ceremony location
- secure gifts / certificates / furnishings
- **Rehearsals for ceremony**
  - practice music
  - practice ceremony
  - practice speeches
- Conduct ceremony

Closing Celebration
- **Reservations**
  - reserve date
  - reserve location

Figure 4-4

Chapter 5:

Studying for the Passage

Study is a lifelong discipline. The study component of the *Orita* program is based on this reality. Any successful adult will engage in study, whether or not he or she is enrolled in a formal educational program. We are writing at the turn of the millennium, and researchers tell us that, because of the rapid pace of change in technology and lifestyle, adults in the future will move through a series of careers, rather than stay in one field. This will mean that adults will have to know how to find information and retrain themselves in new areas, in order to remain marketable.

Studying can take place in many ways, whether alone on a mountaintop observing nature,

97

conversing with a knowledgeable person, conducting a survey on a street corner or in a retail store, developing a financial plan, rehearsing a song, drawing someone's portrait, or the more traditional reading, writing, and calculating. Among all the aspects of any *Orita* project, the Study component is the most extensive. By agreeing to submit to the discipline of *Orita*, a youth commits to engaging in a series of learning activities designed to expand his or her knowledge of self, family origins, ethnic heritage, spiritual principles, and future potential. A key benefit of your youth participating in an *Orita* program is the opportunity for him or her to experience studying as challenging, relevant, enjoyable, and not exclusively done in school.

What must our youth study in order to be prepared for adulthood?

No single ritual or educational activity can cover the entire, awesome task of preparing young black men and women for responsible adulthood. The ideas we used in our program came from a variety of cultural influences, books, ideas, suggestions and the experience of the young people themselves. The ideas you select to implement will depend on the vision and strategies you created as described in the previous chapter.

To begin organizing this phase of the *Orita* project, develop a list of topics which the youth should study. Plan for the youth to use a variety of formats for study. Individual study might include reading books, memorizing wisdom writings, practicing financial strategies, filling an apprenticeship, and conducting research and interviews. Group activities might include visiting places of historical interest, listening to the wisdom of elders, and participating in challenging manual or physical activity. The Study component should last long enough (several weeks or months), so that at the end, when you test the youth in various ways, they will be able to demonstrate that they have grown in the areas you identified as needing strengthening.

The parents in our *Orita* program developed the following list of topics, and organized presentations and discussions about them during the Saturday evening sessions with the youth:

1. personal finances
2. values / principles
3. beauty / image
4. politics
5. African history
6. family responsibility
7. physical development
8. career development
9. community service
10. spirituality

We picked these topics because we had identified them

as areas where there were gaps in our children's formal schooling and where we believed our parental training could use some reinforcement.

At the end of each Saturday evening session, the facilitator gave assignments for the youth to complete on their own, [see Appendix]. We generally did not give due dates for completing assignments. We encouraged the youth to take responsibility for their own learning, working at their own pace and determining the level of effort they would invest. Not every *Orita* youth completed all of these study projects, but we kept track of the activities each youth completed, to make sure that they were all engaged in some reasonable amount of study, and to encourage them to do as many as possible. If a youth felt sufficiently satisfied with the output of his activity, he placed his report, artwork, completed test, or other work product in his *Orita* portfolio, to display to friends and relatives at the closing ceremony.

A key point that *Orita* planners must realize is that the project should empower our youth to take responsibility for their own learning. The study component should have a balance between adult-centered, group learning activities and those in which the students engage individually at their own pace. We have prepared guidelines for facilitators, to help you monitor the effectiveness of your role in the *Orita* study activities, [see Appendix].

**Memorizing principles is an investment
in future success**
In addition to the topics for study, another important aspect of the rites of passage program was memorizing important information from our spiritual and cultural heritage. At each biweekly session, the youth practiced reciting from memory the Apostles' Creed, which many of them had never learned before. They also recited the names of the books of the Bible, in order, as well as Bible passages like "The Lord's Prayer". We memorized the Nguzo Saba, or Seven Principles of Kwanzaa, concepts, which have been and remain critical to the survival and success of people of African descent. Parents also participated in the memorization activity, underscoring the idea that this is information that adults of African descent need to know, even if they had not learned them as a youth. Music and song were very useful in aiding memorization. Our young men adapted a musical rendition of the Nguzo Saba, written in an a cappella style, which they practiced and sang at the closing ceremony.

**A successful adult can handle
physical challenges in nature**
In addition to memorization, research, and writing, our youth had to experience physical challenge as well. The fathers, accompanied by a few other men, organized a mountain climbing trip to Bear Mountain, near

West Point, about 30 miles from our city. An all day hike, the journey required that the young men wear shoes (rather than sneakers) and carry appropriate gear and lunches. They traveled to the starting point in cars and vans. The journey to the top of the mountain was 3,500 feet, and at the top, the group planted a time capsule, a glass thermos, with notes from each of them containing their pledges to themselves and their families. They promised to return in five years for a reunion, and to see if they could unearth the capsule and revisit their pledges in light of their life at that time. Coincidentally, five years later would be at the start of the new millenium, a fitting time for taking stock.

For urban sons (and fathers) who are more comfortable on subways and buses than on dirt roads, the trek was a substantial challenge physical. The young men were surprisingly out of shape, and several endured some pretty grueling physical discomfort on the trip. Some got separated from the group and encountered frightening strangers, before they were reunited. Not only was it physically challenging, but emotionally and spiritually as well.

In almost all rites of passage programs, the physical challenge involves some outdoor experience, often a wilderness experience where the youth are required to spend several hours or even days and nights alone. There are numerous variations on such a theme. In some programs, fasting is part of the physical challenge. In general, such experiences are low-cost activities, since the comforts of food and home are minimized. The major expenses are the cost of transportation to an appropriate, relatively safe location.

In our research on rites of passage around the world, we have found two tests of adulthood to be almost universal. One is the ability to endure physical privation and discomfort, without losing one's composure, self-discipline and focus. The other is the ability to survive outdoors in a completely natural setting for an extended period of time. Even the most hardened street youth, bold in the face of weapons, drugs or high speed locomotion, may find him or herself terrified by a few nights alone in the woods. In fact, we have read reports about several wilderness experience programs, which have had great success in providing life-changing experiences for young adults.

Leaders of the Physical Challenge will find that it is a wonderful tool for demonstrating the relationship between mind, body, and spirit. While the Study Component develops in each Orita youth an awareness and appreciation of the mind, and the Ceremony and Celebration Components address the spiritual aspect of their journey through life, the Physical Challenge heightens the youths' awareness of the need for character, physical strength, and courage.

Regardless of whether you choose to have the youths climb a small mountain or compete in an ath-

letic event, here are some tips you should follow:
- ❑ Create an air of excitement.
- ❑ Protect the youths from any real danger.
- ❑ Scout out the activity site and know the area.
- ❑ Conduct a briefing, complete with maps, charts, time schedules, if needed.
- ❑ Encourage youths who excel to be concerned about others.
- ❑ Encouarge youths who fall behind to learn to keep going.
- ❑ Have a mission objective.
- ❑ Reserve a time when the youths will hear a talk from the leaders.
- ❑ Reserve a time to answer the youths' questions about the experience.
- ❑ Make sure they have plenty to eat.
- ❑ Have fun!

Other Study Component activities, throughout our *Orita* year, provided opportunities for the youth to engage in meaningful study. At the Launch event, youth listened to and reflected on the words of the village elder initiating the year's program, after he individually confirmed that each youth had made a commitment to the program.

Early in the study component, the youth organized a *sou sou*, savings circle, practiced by many cultures, especially African, Caribbean, Asian, and Hispanic immigrants in the United States, who find that discriminatory bank policies often make it difficult for them to get loans for various purposes. In this financial practice, each participant entrusts a fixed sum of money every week, or other time interval, to a trusted member of the community. This trusted individual disburses the pool of money to a different participant, at every time interval, providing the recipient a lump sum of money at his or her turn. Everyone in the savings circle must be trustworthy and live up to his or her commitment to the group. For example, if a participant drops out before everyone else has received a disbursement, the process is seriously disrupted. Although our sons only contributed a few dollars each time, to collect a twenty or thirty dollar disbursement at their turn, they had a valuable experience in teamwork, problem-solving and building trust among their peers.

We took advantage of some school holidays to set up special "study days", where all the *Orita* youth spent "the day" at one parent's house, and, individually and in small groups, worked on their study projects, with fun-filled lunch and recreation breaks. Trips and picnics sometimes provided spontaneous opportunities for group practice and review, as did rehearsals for the closing ceremony.

One of the most important study projects is the *Orita* youth preparing his or her speech for the closing ceremony. Popular psychology tells us that speaking in public can be one of the most stressful tasks that many adults experience in their lives. In his classic, *Public Speaking and Influencing Men in Business*, Dale Carnegie spoke of the importance of training oneself in the art of public speaking, calling it "...one of the best methods ever yet devised to help people eliminate their fears and feelings of inferiority." He continued, "I found that learning to speak in public is nature's own method of overcoming self-consciousness and building up courage and self-confidence. Why? Because speaking in public makes us come to grips with our fears."

Because in our society, so much about us is judged by the way that we present ourselves in speaking, no preparation for adulthood can be complete without giving our youth a quality experience in speechmaking. Youth should begin working on their speech several weeks or months in advance of the closing ceremony. The speech should state the youth's assessment of the *Orita* experience and its benefits for him or her. The speech should reflect their growth and experience of adulthood, and should acknowledge those who have played a part in shaping them. Under no circumstances should an adult write the speech for any *Orita* youth. Youth should practice their speeches repeatedly, to ensure the smoothest possible delivery.

At our son's *Orita* ceremony, each parent (mother and father, or male and female surrogate / guardian) gave a speech on behalf of their youth. For some parents, this may have been as stressful as it was for their son. Samples of the speeches given by *Orita* youth are enclosed in the appendix of the book. Feel free to use ideas in guiding your youth to develop their speeches for your closing program.

No guarantees of mastery

One of the key projects of the Study Component is the youth's scrapbook or portfolio of project reports and completed assignments, and a written speech for delivery at the closing ceremony. Parent reviewers quizzed students to see what they retained from the study projects; the Village Elder interviewed each of them for feedback on their overall experience.

Even with this evaluation process, there is no guarantee that each youth has mastered all of the study material. Youth should not be forbidden to complete the program because they cannot successfully recite from memory one or more of the study items. The idea of any tests should be to hold students accountable and to make them aware of the extent to which they have mastered or not mastered the material.

Obviously, if there are whole aspects of the program which a youth has consistently declined to attempt to master, the youth and his parents should discuss whether or not it is reasonable for him or her to claim completion of the program. However, our youth already have too many opportunities to experience failure in school and other venues. And, how many African-American adults can claim mastery of the known history of people of African descent? However, to move into adulthood without ever having seriously examined this information is a travesty. We believe such knowledge of self is vital for successful adulthood in America in the 21st century. Every attempt should be made to encourage every youth to experience success as an *Orita* participant.

Chapter 6:

Celebrating the Passage

The culmination of the *Orita* process is the closing ceremony, followed immediately by the celebration. These two gatherings can be located in various types of facilities. Some ceremonies are held in the sanctuary of a house of worship, followed by a reception or party in the social hall. Our *Orita* rites were concluded in a catering establishment, where both the ceremony and the celebration could be held in the same location.

Similarly multipurpose facilities are hotel meeting space, a community center, a school auditorium or other gathering space. If you decide to use a catering establishment or restaurant for both, be sure that you can have a reasonable degree of privacy and insulation from the distraction of other groups using the facility. Hotels and catering establishments often will not charge a separate fee for rental of the space, including it in the per person cost of the meal. It may turn out to be less expensive to use such a location than to rent a space and pay separately for catering. On the other hand, if you use a sanctuary for the ceremony, the celebration should probably take place in another location where food, music, laughter and movement are more appropriate. Where weather permits, it might be feasible to have all or part of the observance in an appropriate outdoor space.

Whether in the *Orita* passage or in any other rites of passage program, perhaps the most distinctive feature is the ceremony. The entire yearlong process culminates in this closing ritual. The ceremony has to reflect the values that are important to the families involved. It has to be appropriate to the community, the culture, and the age of the youth involved.

In the appendix, you will find the ceremony that we used, culled and adapted from a variety of sources. We drew on different cultures, on similar rites of passage programs. Your ceremony should be adapted from this or similar material, but not be followed blindly. The ritual should be meaningful, most of all, to the youth involved.

Although communities and families will develop the ceremony in different ways, we expect that, over time, some aspects will become standard *Orita* practice. One such practice is opening the ceremony with the *Orita* youth clearly stating his or her purpose for participating in the ceremony: to announce that he or she is ready to pass from childhood into responsible adulthood. This announcement of purpose can be ritualized and stylized in many ways; but the key is to establish that this event is initiated by the youth, and that, by so doing, he or she is connecting to a long line of ancestors who have already taken their responsible places in life.

In the *Orita* ceremony for our son, the first words spoken were an exchange between the Village Elder and the *Orita* youth:

Elder: Who is it that comes to the *Orita* passage?
***Orita* Youth:** "It is I, John Kwasi Jackson, son of _____ and ____, grandson of _____, _____, _____, and _____", stating his full name and the names of his ancestors.
Elder: "Why have you come?"
***Orita* Youth:** "I have completed the requirements and I am here to take my place....."

We dramatized the opening by having the parents symbolically release their youth, done without words, with only the sound of African drums in the background. The young men stood, waiting their turn, at one end of the room, while holding an unlit candle. We used candles to symbolize the new phase of life that the *Orita* youth would enter that day. One family at a

111

time, the parents (or surrogate parents) entered the room from the opposite side, and walked down an aisle toward their son, the parents carrying a lighted candle. Half way down the aisle, the parents and son met. The youth took his candle and lit it from the flame of his parents' candle, then turned and walked toward the Village Elder to declare his readiness for the new level of responsibility. The parents then took their seats.

This opening ritual dramatized the parents' important but diminishing role, giving their son over to manhood, and to the scrutiny of the community and the Village Elder. The youth goes to face the challenge of adulthood, leaving behind, to some extent, his parents, and declares that he wants to enter the passage. Throughout the ceremony, the youth's candle remained lit, sitting in a kinara (Kwanzaa candleholder) on a table at the front of the room. [See appendix for *Orita* ceremony ritual].

There are many variations of this ritual. For example, in a ceremony for a single child, the parents might be augmented by grandparents, godparents, sisters and brothers, and other members of the extended family, all or some carrying lit candles. Depending on safety considerations and availability, all the candles of the adults could be left lit for the entire ceremony, while the youth's candle joins those of his elders.

The tone of the event can be upbeat or serious. The use of drums, other instrumental music, live or prerecorded music, and vocalists with or without accompaniment is a matter of individual preference and taste. To help ensure that your ceremony is most relevant, your youth and his caregivers should talk about what's going on in their lives and develop a ritual that best reflects that experience.

Attendees should be people of every age and relationship to the youth, who care. Relatives, friends, adults, children, people from the community, - all are saying, "I'm interested. I'm going to be here for you as you move into adulthood. I'm going to pray for this young person."

If the family is living away from most of its relatives and close friends, it might be desirable to plan the ceremony at the local church, immediately after a Sunday morning worship service. The congregation can be invited in advance to participate, similar to a christening ceremony. The pastor's role, not unlike the role in a wedding, would have been developed and rehearsed ahead of time.

Families who have reunions might include an *Orita* ceremony and celebration in their festivities. It would be beneficial for youth and adults for the family to feature an *Orita* ceremony and celebration at their national gatherings. If it's not possible to include the full ceremony in the reunion schedule, a formal acknowledgement or blessing on the youth in the family who have been through the experience since the last reunion would give support to the practice or rites of passage.

Well before the ceremony, identify key individuals, to speak, sing or pray on behalf of various groups represented. Very significant individuals should be asked to prepare brief but personal remarks: the mother (or surrogate), the father (or surrogate), a young adult who has successfully passed through a rites of passage experience, the youth's minister or spiritual adviser.

The speech by Orita youth

A highlight of the event should be a presentation by each *Orita* candidate. At minimum, each youth should recite a prepared speech, thoroughly edited and rehearsed, that demonstrates his/her ability to communicate verbally. In their speeches, your youth may share what being an American of African descent means to them, how they have grown during the *Orita* process, or their aspirations and vision of adulthood. A sample speech by one of our youth, written when he was twelve, appears in the Appendix.

Another presentation by the youth in our celebration was a chant of the Seven Principles in Swahili and in English, which they sang a capella, in contemporary style, adapted from a recording by William Gilbert Emanuel, producer of the book and videotape series, *People of Color in the Bible*. We would caution against turning the event into a display of indi-

114

vidual talent; save that for other venues. The emphasis here should relate directly to the theme of the *Orita* rites of passage.

Choose Scripture verses that are meaningful to the families and have them read at various points during the program. Songs, like the Black National Anthem are very meaningful for the ceremony. Other hymns, for example Negro spirituals - speak to our struggle and victory, to having goals in life, and to the value of charting a course. These songs are particularly appropriate. Poetry with similar themes can also be read.

The organizers should seriously consider inviting the local press to cover the event. Alternatively, someone who is knowledgeable about preparing press releases, and can take crisp, clear photographs of the event, should prepare a press release for one or more local newspapers. The media was interested in our program, and the newspaper photo and story that appeared in our community newspaper provided memorable documentation of the occasion.

The youth should be presented with some tangible mementos of the rites of passage program. Rev. Fair suggested having medallions made with an *Orita* symbol or insignia engraved on them. One person we know collected gold jewelry from various members of their family, had it melted down and fashioned into a special gold medallion for their son. Of course, this can be quite costly. We advise you not to overemphasize the material value of this memento. The graphic in Figure 6-1 is inspired by Rev. Frank Fair's *Orita* logo. You may use it to design your *Orita* medallion, invitations, T-shirts and other materials. It features the crossroads of life which the youth are facing, the scriptures and the cross which guide and give hope, and the drum of celebration, a symbol of our cultural heritage.

Figure 6-1

In our case, rather than use precious metals, we presented our sons with a very elegant New Testament, complete with Psalms and Proverbs, gold colored edged pages, and a strip of kente cloth. We also presented a certificate with the youth's name in it, and signed by the presiding elder, certifying to his successful completion of the program.

Again, there are variations on this idea; woodcarvings, quilts or other handcrafted items can be customized. These should include the date, the name of the youth, and the symbol of the program. Each youth can then leave the event with something in his or her hand, to commemorate the event.

One suggestion is to ask the youth to pledge to take care of the memento, and to carry on the tradition by having a rites of passage ceremony for his son or daughter in the future, presenting him or her with the medallion or other memento.

Prepare, prepare, and prepare!
Preparation is the key to a successful ceremony. Give all the participants adequate notice, even if only to read a Scripture verse or poem, so that it can be delivered fluently and with the desired impact. Give soloist(s) time to practice too. A full dress rehearsal with everyone may not be possible; but at least one hour before the start of the program, every participant should be present and ready to appear, to eliminate delays. Flaws in timing will stymie the celebration. On the other hand, precise execution will allow participants time to express themselves in a variety of ways.

There are also all sorts of ways to build in drama, without boring everyone to tears. Our closing ceremony had lots of features, including litanies, rituals, prayers, charges, pledges; and all performed within about 90 minutes. That may sound long, but remember, we were celebrating seven youth at the same time. If several youth are in the program, I would caution the organizers not to encourage unnecessary competition for "the best" skill or accomplishment. This is not a competitive event. Youth get enough of that in school. If every youth has completed the *Orita* course of study and work, then every youth should share equally in the celebration. The real competition comes as the young adult squares off against the forces that seek to prevent a successful passage to adulthood. The congregation and the community are a resource for every youth, to help ensure that he or she makes it.

A festive celebration

Although the entire closing program is a celebration, we distinguish the festive part from the more formal ceremonial part. Give careful thought and planning to these festivities.

Most celebrations include some eating, but the food should not be extravagant or wasteful. If you reserve a restaurant or catering hall, where there is a fixed price per person, you will have to plan carefully to limit the number of persons you invite, so that you don't exceed your budget. A catered meal makes for a more formal and elegant occasion; it can be buffet, family-style or restaurant style. The meal, depending on the time of day and location, can be breakfast, brunch, lunch, or dinner. A well executed brunch can feature all cold foods, breads, condiments, fruits, juices, soft drinks, or a combination of hot and cold items. There are a number of options for providing a meal. Parents can prepare the food, friends can bring specific dishes, and a caterer can serve it at a catering or restaurant establishment. Again, we believe strongly that it is desirable that if you hire catering services that you do so with a well-run, community-based business, exemplifying the seven principles (Nguzo Saba).

Some youth will want to have a teen-aged style party, with popular music, or games, or dancing, and with only minimal food and sodas. Some families may decide to conduct the celebration somewhat like a wedding or fancy birthday party, with speeches, toasts, and formal eating, where adults and youth participate in all activities.

Whatever form the celebration takes, it should be consistent with the principles of *Orita* and demonstrate the state of responsible adulthood that the youth has committed to that day. When the day has come to an end, all who have attended should remember the ceremony as vividly and positively as they do the celebration afterwards.

How do we celebrate the passage? When people think of a celebration they often think visually, about special clothing, decor, foods, gifts, people, and dancing. We've listed in the Appendix materials and resources that you may use to enhance not only the celebration, but also all phases of the *Orita* program. Certainly, these aids complement the more intangible aspects of the celebration discussed above. The possibilities are probably endless for using your creativity to create a memory that your youth and your community will recall for years to come.

Epilogue:

Institutionalizing Orita

After your young man or woman's passage into adulthood has been celebrated by a formal rites ceremony, what then?

At the time of this writing, nearly five years after our son's *Orita* program, one of the six youths who completed the program with him was in a residential, rehabilitation program for troubled youth. We still have hope that he will be physically and spiritually able to make the return trip to the mountaintop after the turn of the millenium. Even during the program, there were signs that he was having trouble submitting to the *Orita* disciplines. Did *Orita* fail for him? We think not. His transition to responsible adulthood has been stormy, but we believe that *Orita* has

121

and will make a difference in the quality of his life.

In spite of all the prayers and pledges that are typically made at the ceremony, it is unlikely that your son or daughter will walk a perfect path into adulthood. Some of our youth will make serious detours, and some may stray permanently from their commitment. The rites of passage program and ceremony will not make up for dysfunctional family relationships, inconsistent and destructive lifestyles, unrestrained influence of negative peer group; the list goes on and on.

However, those of us who live by Biblical faith, hold firmly to the promise in, Proverbs 22:6, that if we train up our child in the way (s)he should go, when (s)he is old, (s)he will not depart from it. Training is what the Study Component is all about.

Furthermore, by publicly demonstrating your convictions in a celebration for your own child's passage, you may literally save the lives of other youth—who are either in attendance, or whose parents attend and become motivated to emulate what you have done. In fact, the major reason for this book is to document our own experience and to assist other families who have a desire to do something similar. Next to seeing our own son live out the values committed to in his rites of passage observance, our strongest desire is to see the practice become institutionalized in our community.

As people of the African Diaspora, cut off from our ancestry by the Middle Passage and slavery, we have found it difficult to rebuild our cultural traditions. Unlike those European descendants who are treated like celebrities when they speak in European language accents and identify with European culture, African Americans who attempt to reconnect culturally with their African origins experience a range of negative responses from those espousing assimilation. We believe, however, that the person who can most effectively assimilate is the person who has a healthy self-concept. And, in spite of all the progress we have made, generation after generation of our youth still find their self-esteem assaulted by the never-ending cycles of resurgent racism, white supremacy, and Eurocentrism.

So, how do we use modern techniques to build institutions, to help ourselves? First, we need to agree on what to call this developing institution. The rites-of-passage process needs a standard name that is widely recognized in our communities—regardless of regional, denominational and socioeconomic differences. The generic "rites of passage" is too unwieldy for greeting cards and logos. The name *"Orita,"* Yoruba for "Crossroads", was used by Dr. Frank Fair, and is easy to pronouce, taps into our common African roots, and is free from preconceived, negative associations. The name should not be copyrighted or protected for private use. We have used it freely in this text, to continue the work which Dr. Fair began in the 1970's.

Secondly, some common logo, or color scheme will help to give rapid recognition and promote the idea of celebration, which people naturally love to do. Like the growth of the Kwanzaa observance, the manufacture of greeting cards, gifts, and artifacts associated with the *Orita* ceremony will help to give it longevity, as participants retain memorabilia from their ceremonies as they move on in adulthood.

Eventually, families will tend to standardize on an age at which youth will enter rites of passage. If that age is not younger than 12 and preferably not older than 16, youth will look forward to the experience and parents' planning will be easier. Community leaders and organizations will offer facilities and services; entrepreneurs will offer package deals.

Our family has committed to creating and manufacturing materials to help other families participate in *Orita* rites of passage. We use the medium of the Internet to provide access to a current list of items which we have in stock. Customized items can be produced on request.

Appendix I

Orita Study
Component Materials

Sample homework assignments / projects

1) Economics - Family Budget
• Write out your family's expenses for one month. Parents should allow young men to see the statements for the major bills for the last month. (This assignment is NOT to be shared outside the family. However, parents will be asked to verify that the assignment is completed)
• Write out a week's grocery expenses - and do the family shopping for one week.

2) Swahili - Nguzo Saba - write out the 7 Swahili words and their English translations.

3) Bible facts and Bible books
Memorize the 4 types of books in the Old Testament and the 4 types in the New. Know how many books

are in each type. Know the names of the books, in order, in each type [see below]

4) Family Tree

Write out first and last names of all known ancestors, back to the 8 great grandparents. Do not include cousins. Only parents, grandparents (4), great grandparents, uncles / aunts, great uncles / great aunts.

Arrange them in a chart in the format we discussed - father's parents on one side and mother's on the other.

Then prepare to do a final drawing, with all boxes of even size.

5) Personal Testimony

Write out what becoming a man means to you, and how you have grown or changed since being in the Orita program.

6) Autobiography

Write an outline for a brief autobiography (2-4 pages), listing important events in your life, and describing them in more detail in the actual autobiography.

7) Future Vision

Write about your picture of yourself in 5 years. What will you look like? where will you be living? what will you be doing? how will you be supported? who will be your associates? what will you have accomplished?

Make a detailed sketch to match this future vision.

Repeat the above for how you will look in 10

years.

8) Letters to elected representatives / Community Service
• Write the names and addresses of your elected representatives (City Councilperson, State Senator, State Assemblyperson, US Congressperson, US Senator, Mayor, Governor, President). Describe some problems in your community that you would like to see acted on - and let your representatives know how you feel about it, in a letter to each one.
•Do some volunteer work for an individual or organization in your community, other than your regular church ministry or activity. Describe what you did and how you felt after doing it.

9) Black experience in America
• Look through magazines and books and clip or photocopy articles / pictures which illustrate the black experience in America - both good and bad aspects of this experience, if possible.
• Write a brief report on an African-American role model, in an area other than sports or entertainment, whom you admire. Explain why you admire him or her.

10) Map of Africa
Fill in the names of all the nations on a map of Africa. (You should also be able to draw a freehand map of Africa, and locate most of the major countries on it.)

11) Book reports on books by African-American authors

Write a one-page report on at least one book by an African-American author, which reflects some aspect of the experience of people of African descent in America.

12) Africans in the Bible

Write the names of 7 people in the Bible of directly African origin, and the Scripture verses / passages where you can read about them.

13) Interview with elder

Interview a black man who is over 65 years old. Find out (and write down) what life was like when he was young? How were blacks treated then? What does he feel are the major challenges facing young black men in the future?

14) Physical Challenge

Accept and complete the physical challenge the Orita fathers are preparing for you.

15) Portfolio

Design a scrapbook or portfolio for display at the closing ceremony. Decide what you will put in it that reveals your personal experience - photos? clippings? reports? letters from people? creations?

16) *Sou-Sou* Savings Circle

This exercise is rooted in West Africa and builds on trust and teamwork to accumulate money. Find and interview someone in your community who has participated in a Caribbean-style *sou-sou,* or similar savings circle. Work with other *Orita* youth to organize your own savings circle, without adult intervention.

Decide how much your regular contributions will be. Select one among you to collect and pay out funds. Agree on the rules of your *sou sou*, and operate it at least until each participant has had one turn to collect.

Important Information to Memorize
NGUZO SABA
(7 Principles)
UMOJA - UNITY
Standing together, believing in each other, familyhood
KUJICHAGULIA- SELF DETERMINATION
Live up to your own expectations, follow the traditions that help us define ourselves, keep going until you reach your goal
UJIMA - COLLECTIVE WORK AND RESPONSIBILITY
Working together and supporting the efforts of others
UJAMAA - COOPERATIVE ECONOMICS
Putting our monies together to create our own wealth for our future and our children's futures
NIA - PURPOSE
Knowing that you are valuable and that you are here for a purpose which you can achieve
KUUMBA - CREATIVITY
Using your God-given imagination and mind, expressing yourself
IMANI - FAITH

Believing that good will happen, putting your trust in God

The Apostle's Creed
I believe in God the Father, Almighty, Maker of heaven and earth;
And in Jesus Christ, his only Son, our Lord;
Who was conceived by the Holy Ghost, born of the Virgin Mary,
Suffered under Pontius Pilate, was crucified, dead and buried;
He descended into hell; the third day He arose again from the dead;
He ascended into heaven, and sitteth at the right hand of God the Father Almighty'
From thence He shall come to judge the quick and the dead.
I believe in the Holy Ghost, the Holy Church of Jesus Christ,
The communion of saints, the forgiveness of sins, the resurrection of the body, and the life everlasting.
Amen.

Books of the Bible
5 books of Law
Genesis, Exodus, Leviticus, Numbers, Deuteronomy
12 books of history
Joshua, Judges, Ruth, 1st Samuel, 2nd Samuel, 1st Kings, 2nd Kings, 1st Chronicles, 2nd Chronicles, Ezra, Nehemiah, Esther

5 books of poetry

Job, Psalms, Proverbs, Ecclesiastes, Song of Solomon

17 books of prophecy

Isaiah, Jeremiah, Lamentations, Ezekiel, Daniel, Hosea, Joel, Amos, Obadiah, Jonah, Micah, Nahum, Habakkuk, Zephaniah, Haggai, Zechariah, Malachi

= = =

39 Books in the Old Testament

4 Gospels

Matthew, Mark, Luke, John

1 Book of History

Acts

21 Letters

Romans, 1st Corinthians, 2nd Corinthians, Galatians, Ephesians, Philippians, Colossians, 1st Timothy, 2nd Timothy, Titus, 1st Thessalonians, 2nd Thessalonians, Philemon, Hebrews, James, 1st Peter, 2nd Peter, 1st John, 2nd John, 3rd John, Jude

1 Book of Prophecy

Revelation

= = =

27 Books in the New Testament

= = = =

66 Books in the Bible

Guidelines for facilitating study activities

For the parent / facilitator who is not a professional

educator - here's a crash course from the field of education. This is adapted from Dr. Joyce F. Baynes, as developed and taught to faculty in the Teaneck and Englewood, New Jersey public schools. Anyone facilitating Orita project activities, especially in the study component should monitor his or her effectiveness with youth, according to these criteria.

If good instruction is going on, the following four aspects should be visible in the learning situation:

Purpose
Relationships
Strategies
Feedback

Purpose - The workshop leader clearly explains to the young people the purpose of the lesson, activity, or exercise. The purpose should fit into the mission of the program. If there is not a clear connection, perhaps it is not worthy of the limited time resource we have to spend on it.

Relationships - Each youth must feel connected to the workshop leader. There should be a feeling of relatedness between them. To be effective as a facilitator, he or she must ensure that no youth is alienated by sensing favoritism, bias, or hostility. Facilitators must be sensitive to the nonverbal communication they give the group about the worth of each student. Overt factors that prevent a feeling of relatedness are criticisms, bringing up past behavior, put-downs, insults, ridicule of all, any student or group of students. Subtle factors that undermine relatedness are comments that reveal low expectations of some students, favoring boys over girls or vice versa, waiting longer for one child to try to come up with an answer or a statement, while rushing another one of whom less is expected, touching or standing closer to one student and keeping distance from another, etc.

Strategies - The teacher must have a quiver full of arrows, a toolkit full of strategies that will allow every student to participate fully. Diverse strategies which will also keep every student engaged and using as many as possible of the several intelligences which modern thinkers believe we each have. Instruction must not exclusively use one strategy. Lecturing should be used sparingly. Group work should be used more, although not slavishly, music and movement, other senses must get involved, writing - journaling, not fill-in-the-blank, boring "school-like" exercises. A variety of instructional strategies within the lesson and among the various lessons will make students look forward to the study component.

Feedback - It is important that we adults cherish feedback from our youth. Comments that reveal attitudes we don't espouse or appreciate must be accepted as valuable for instruction, for teachable moments, and not for opportunities for criticism or put-down. "Mistakes" must be embraced - both by the facilitator and the youthful participant - this applies to mistakes in a variety of contexts: intellectual, music, movement, spiritual, etc. feedback we get from students. Use a variety of means to generate feedback - paper and pencil tests are possible, but should not be overused. Journals that allow students to describe their feelings and recollections are generally more telling, and interesting to read. Other forms of feedback are reports, dramatizations, skits, research projects, letters, artwork, musical compositions - raps: all of these means tell us how much our students have really internalized and how they are processing the information.

Appendix II

A Sample Orita Ceremony

Musical Prelude
If any, background music recorded / instrumental:

Congregational Song
a capella - Minister leading) "Amazing Grace"

Processional
[Parents form a processional bearing lighted candles, entering from the rear. The first two parents walk from the rear to the middle of aisle and wait. Their son approaches from the front and meets them, taking their candle and walking to the altar, while his parents stand behind until he has

135

been questioned by the minister. Son places his candle in candleholder, then stands at the free-standing microphone, facing the minister.]

Minister
Who is it that comes to the Ceremony of the Crossroads?

Son
It is I,_____, son of _____ and _____the children of _____ and _____, _____ and _____the children of _____ and _____, _____ and _____, _____ and _____, and _____ and _____.

Minister
Why do you come?

Son:
I come because I am of the age of consciousness and, having been given these tasks, I have completed my assignments, and I desire God's blessings and the blessings of this religious community.

Minister
(turning to the congregation) What do you say to this request?

Congregation
(standing) Let it be so! Amen!

Parents
(Parents take their seats in the congregation, front row. Minister signals to next family to come forward and repeats. When all are finished, minister signals to them to take their seats on the platform, facing the congregation).

Minister

(Scripture readings) Remember your Creator in the days of your youth, before the days of trouble come and the years approach when you will say, "I find no pleasure in them". (Ecclesiastes 12:1)

Now all has been heard; here is the conclusion of the matter. Fear God and keep his commandments, for this is the whole duty of man. For God will bring every deed into judgment, including every hidden thing, whether it be good or evil. (Ecclesiastes 12:13-14)

Minister
Let us pray (prayer of direction)
Eternal God, ...
Let them always strive to know and to do Thy will.
Amen.

Solo:
"Your Reflection"

Minister
Does this body have anything to say to the
young men?

(Congregation and sons stand; congregation recites
together to the sons)
Congregation
DO YOUR UTMOST TO PRESENT YOURSELF
EACH DAY TO GOD, AS A WORKMAN WITH
NOTHING TO BE ASHAMED OF. BE SURE TO
TELL THE TRUTH AT ALL TIMES WHEN
YOU SPEAK. BE SURE TO SHUN EMPTY
SPEECHES THAT VIOLATE WHAT IS HOLY,
REFRAIN FROM EVIL AND AVOID EVILDO-
ERS, FOR THEY WILL ADVANCE TO MORE
AND MORE UNGODLINESS. SEEK PEACE AT
ALL TIMES. REGARDLESS OF THE AD-
VANCE IN TECHNOLOGY, THE FEAR OF
GOD IS THE BEGINNING OF WISDOM.

Minister
Young men, what is your confession of faith?

Sons
(Together) - recite The Apotles' Creed

I believe in God the Father, Almighty,
Maker of heaven and earth
And in Jesus Christ, His only Son, our Lord;
who was conceived by the Holy Ghost, born of the
Virgin Mary
suffered under Pontius Pilate, was crucified, dead
and buried
He descended into hell; the third day He arose
again from the dead
He ascended into heaven, and sittetch at the right
hand of God the Father Almighty
From thence He shall come to judge the quick and
the dead.
I believe in the Holy Ghost, the Holy Church of
Jesus Christ,
The communion of saints, the forgiveness of sins,
the resurrection of the body, and the life everlasting.
Amen.

Minister
Sons, what are your prayers?

Sons
(individually)

Son #1
Lord, I pray for understanding.

Congregation
Lord, grant him understanding.

Son #2
Lord, I pray for wisdom.

Congregation
Lord, grant him wisdom.

Son #3
Lord, I pray to live righteously.

Congregation
Let him live righteously.

Son #4
Lord, I pray for spiritual strength.

Congregation
Lord, grant him spiritual strength.

Son #5
Lord, I pray for faith.

Congregation
Lord grant him faith.

Son #6
Lord, I pray for self-control.

Congregation
Lord, grant him self-control.

Son #7
Lord, I pray for courage.

Congregation
Lord, grant him courage to live a godly life. For you require of us as we walk between the cradle and the grave to love mercy, do justly, and to walk humbly before You. Amen! Amen! Amen!

Soloist
(leads the congregation in singing) AMEN

Youthful Friend
Challenge by youthful friend

Reading:
Poem "I Loved My Africa" by Etta Ladson

Mothers
(One at a time, each mother goes to the free standing mike and addresses her son; he stands and moves toward her, and resumes his seat after she is finished.)

Reading: (one of the Fathers)

"I AM The Black Man" by Dr. Nathan Hare

Fathers
(One at a time, each father goes to the free standing mike and addresses his son; the son stands and moves toward him, and resumes his seat after he is finished. When father is finished, he takes a standing position behind his son's chair, remaining on the platform)

Sons
(All sons kneel down before the altar. They blindfold themselves - symbolizing the unknown future. They silently ponder the future they will take.)

Minister
Will any minister in the congregation come forward to join in prayer for the young men, as we are led by Rev. _____ from _____, West Africa?

Ministers
(The ministers and elders in the congregation come forward and lay hands on the sons)

African Minister
Prayer in African language

Fathers
(Each father removes the blindfold from his son as the son stands up, and drapes the kente cloth around his neck)

Fathers together:
This cloth symbolizes our ancestry in Africa, and receiving it on this day should remind you that you are blessed because of the prayers of your predecessors and their visions of the future. Do you promise to remember its symbolism, wearing it well, and make the best choices that you can make, never bringing shame on your head, this religious community, or above all, on your God?

Sons (together)
I do.

Fathers (together)
Should you marry and have a child, will you consider passing this Orita tradition on to him or her?

Sons (together)
I will.

143

Sons (singing together):
Nguzo Saba Song

Self determination, Unity
Collective Work, Responsibility
Cooperative Economics

Self determination, Purpose
Creativity, and Faith

Ku-ji-cha-gulia, Umoja
Uji-ma Uja- maa
Kujichagulia, Nia
Kuumba, Imani

Sons Words:
Son #1
**(Reads prepared speech at lectern followed by #2
and so on)**

. . .

Minister
Before we conclude, we want to acknowledge those
of our foreparents who have paved the way for us
and returned to God who made them. Let us remember, David Walker, Harriet Tubman, So-

journer Truth, Dr. Martin Luther King, Jr., [followed by list of names of grandparents of sons in the program]

Minister
[Minister says own words of exhortation to the young men, then concludes below]

In conclusion, I present to each of you a certificate documenting this day and a copy of the book of the Proverbs from the Holy Scriptures, to guide you as go forth into manhood.
Read it daily, and meditate on God's words, and your way will be successful.
(To each son in turn:)
[name of Son #1], we welcome you to the honored realm, challenges and responsibilities of black manhood." (Minister hands son a certificate and Bible portion)

[name of Son #2] we welcome you...
[and so on through Son #7]

Let us rise and sing our Black National Anthem as we prepare for the celebration.

Congregation
 Lift Every Voice and Sing

Lift Every Voice And Sing

Lift ev-'ry voice and sing,
Till earth and heaven ring,
Ring with the har-mo-nies of Lib-er-ty;
Let our re-joic-ing rise
High as the list'ning skies,
Let it re-sound loud as the roll-ing sea

Sing a song full of the faith that the dark past has taught us;
Sing a song full of the hope that the pres-ent has brought-us;

Fac-ing the ris-ing sun
Of our new day be-gun,
Let us march on till vic-to-ry - is won.

God of our wea-ry years, God of our silent tears,
Thou who hast
Brought us thus far on - the way;

Thou who hast by thy might, led us into the-light, keep us
For-ev-er in the path, we pray.

Lest our feet stray from the pla-ces,
Our God, where we met Thee,
Lest our hearts, drunk with the wine of the world,
we for-get-Thee;
Shad-owed be-neath Thy hand,
May we for-ev-er-stand,
True to our God,
True to our na-tive land.

Sample Speech by Orita Youth (Age 13)

First of all I would like to thank God for giving me good times and helping me through hard times up to this important point in my life. I would also like to thank my parents for raising me with love and discipline all through my life. Special thanks to all the people in Ebenezer, with whom I grew up with and who molded my personality and spirit. Thank you.

I have accomplished many things in my long thirteen years on this earth. I have become an experienced player of the violin, a very good artist, an athlete, an academic success. Much of this I owe to my parents for their persistence, encouragement, and for believing in me.

I have travelled to many places, Texas, Barbados, New Hampshire, North Carolina, Florida, Ohio, Washington D.C., Connecticut, Virginia, the list goes on. I have also travelled to important landmarks like the White House and the Washington Monument.

My study of black history through books like *Black Boy, To Be a Slave, Raisin in the Sun, To Kill a Mockingbird* and through studying people like Malcolm X, Frederick Douglass, and Reverend Doctor Martin Luther King Junior, I have come to understand the injustices that exist in this country. I have also learned about the disappointments and triumphs of a community due to hard work and persistence. Perhaps the most important and useful thing I have learned is that as a black man, I must make more sacrifices and work to my absolute best ability, in order to be a success. I have also come to this conclusion because Jesus said in Luke 2:48 "From everyone who has been given much, much will be demanded, and from the one who has been entrusted with much, much more will be asked."

In my later life, I hope to be a prominent black leader in the community I decide to live in. I would hope to help young people of African descent to graduate from high school and get a good college education. I want to unlock myths and fears about black people and show the beauty of the African American people to the ignorant.

Up to this point in my life I have had many feelings, feelings of hate, happiness, confusion and sorrow. I have always had dreams of what I could do with my life, but now I realize that I cannot do all of these things. I have wanted to be a lawyer, an astronaut, a doctor, and a marine biologist. Whichever profession I choose, I realize that the most important thing is being a responsible, African American, Christian man.

Bibliography

Emanuel, William Gilbert. *People of Color in the Bible*. Schuylkill Haven, Pennsylvania: Faith of Jesus Center, 1992.

Fair, Frank T. *Orita for Black Youth: An Initiation Into Christian Adulthood*. Valley Forge, Pennsylvania: Judson Press, 1977.

Goggins, Lathardus II. *African Centered Rites of Passage and Education*. Chicago, Illinois: African American Images, 1996.

Hare, Nathan and Julia Hare. *Bringing the Black Boy to Manhood: the passage*. San Francisco, California, The Black Think Tank, 1985.

Hartmann, Thom. *Beyond ADD: Hunting for Reasons in the Past and Present*. Grass Valley, California: Underwood Books, 1996.

Hartmann, Thom. *ADD Success Stories: A Guide to Fulfillment for Families with Attention Deficit Disorder.* Grass Valley, California: Underwood Books, 1995.

Hill, Paul Jr. *Coming of Age: African American Male Rites-Of-Passage.* Chicago, Illinois: African American Images, 1992.

Kunjufu, Jawanza. *Countering the Conspiracy to Destroy Black Boys.* Chicago: African American Images, 1983.

_____. *Critical Issues in Educating African American Youth.* Chicago: African American Images, 1989.

Ladson, Etta May. *Strange Land Songs.* Laurelton, New York: Jewelgate Press, 1991.

Leneman, Cantor Helen, ed. *Bar / Bat Mitzvah Basics.* Woodstock, Vermont: Jewish Light Publishing, 1996.

Lewis, Mary C. *Herstory: Black Female Rites of Passage.* Chicago, Illinois: African American Images, 1988.

Mahdi, Louise Carus, Nancy Geyer Christopher, and Michael Meade, eds. *Crossroads: The Quest for Contemporary Rites of Passage.* La Salle, Illinois: Open Court, 1996.

McKean, Paul, Jeannie McKean, and Maggie Bruehl. *Leading a Child to Independence: A Positive Approach to Raising Children*

Through the Teens. San Bernardino, California: Here's Life Publishers, Inc., 1986.

McKissic, William Dwight, Sr. *Beyond Roots: In Search of Blacks in the Bible*. Wenonah, New Jersey: Renaissance Productions, 1990.

Rutter, Virginia Beane. *Celebrating Girls: Nurturing and Empowering Our Daughters*. Berkeley, California: Conari Press, 1996.

Sheehy, Gail. *New Passages: Mapping Your Life Across Time*. New York: Random House, 1995.

Tatum, Beverly. *"Why Are All the Black Kids Sitting Together in the Cafeteria" And Other Conversations About Race*. New York: Harper Collins, 1997.

Terry, Rod. *Kwanzaa:The Seven Principles*. White Plains, New York: Peter Pauper Press, Inc., 1996.

About the Authors

Marilyn C. Maye is Assistant Superintendent of Schools in Englewood, New Jersey. Born and reared in Harlem, New York City, she is a graduate of Swarthmore College, with degrees in mathematics and in anthropology-sociology, with a concentration in Black Studies. She earned a Master of Arts in Teaching from Harvard Graduate School of Education and a Master of Arts in Mathematical Statistics from Columbia University Graduate School of Arts and Sciences.

After teaching mathematics in the public schools of New York City, Mrs. Maye also taught mathematics in the City University of New York for many years. Pursuing an interest in technology, she entered graduate studies in computer science and later spent several years in New York City government, first as an information systems consultant and eventually as an Assistant Commissioner of the Department of Information Technology and Telecommunications.

While Marilyn and her husband reared Richard, their only child, she returned to the field of education to find the answer to the question, "how should parents and teachers prepare African–American youth for successful adulthood in a stubbornly color–conscious society?"

Warren L. Maye is Assistant Literary Secretary for The Salvation Army's USA Eastern Territory, headquartered in Nyack, N.Y. He is a writer and managing editor of *Good News!* and *¡Buenas Noticias!* newspapers and is contributing editor and writer for *Priority!* magazine. He is currently writing the 127–year history of African Americans in The Salvation Army.

Originally from Cleveland, Ohio, Mr. Maye earned degrees in the field of communication. He graduated from The New School for Social Research (now New School University) and Parsons School of Design, where he earned a Bachelor of Fine Arts, majoring in commercial art with a minor in sociology. He later earned a Master of Arts in Communications from Fordham University Graduate School of Arts and Sciences.

Warren has worked in publishing for more than 20 years. He has designed high school science and history textbooks for Harper & Row Publishers (now

HarperCollins) and Random House Publishers, film-strips and teachers' guides at Youth Education Inc., and industry periodicals for Fairchild Publications, Harcourt Brace–Javanovitch (now Harcourt Brace), and Dun & Bradstreet Inc.

During the late 1970s, Warren and Marilyn published the National Drum, *a faith–based Harlem community magazine dedicated to exploring issues of concern to the black community but not covered by the mainstream media. Since that time, the Mayes have dedicated their lives to making a difference in the world.*

When you have eaten and are satisfied,
praise the Lord your God....
Be careful that you do not forget the Lord your
God, failing to observe his commands,
his laws and his decrees....
Otherwise, when you eat and are satisfied, when
you build fine houses and settle down, and when
your herds and flocks grow large and your silver
and gold increase and all you have is multiplied,
then your heart will become proud
and you will forget the Lord your God,
who brought you out of ...the land of slavery....
You may say to yourself,
'My power and the strength of my hands have
produced this wealth for me.'
But remember the Lord your God, for it is he
who gives you the ability to produce wealth....
If you ever forget the Lord your God...
you will surely be destroyed."

from Deuteronomy 8:10-19,
New International Version